John Milton's

PARADISE LOST

A CONTEMPORARY
LITERARY VIEWS BOOK

Edited and with an Introduction by
HAROLD BLOOM

First Printing

1 3 5 7 9 8 6 4 2

Cover illustration: Detail of *Adam and Eve Driven Out of Paradise, Book 12, line 641* (1827) by John Martin in *Illustrations to Milton's Paradise Lost* Yale Center for British Art, Paul Mellon Collection

Library of Congress Cataloging-in-Publication Data

John Milton's Paradise lost / edited and with an introduction by Harold Bloom.
p. cm. — (Bloom's Notes)
Includes bibliographical references and index.
ISBN 0-7910-4073-9
1. Milton, John, 1608–1674. Paradise lost. 2. Epic poetry, English— History and criticism. 3. Fall of man in literature. I. Bloom, Harold. II. Series.
PR3562.J63 1995
821'.4—dc20
95-43497
CIP

Chelsea House Publishers
1974 Sproul Road, Suite 400
P.O. Box 914
Broomall, PA 19008-0914

Contents

User's Guide

This volume is designed to present biographical, critical, and bibliographical information on John Milton and *Paradise Lost*. Following Harold Bloom's introduction, there appears a detailed biography of the author, discussing the major events in his life and his important literary works. Then follows a thematic and structural analysis of the work, in which significant themes, patterns, and motifs are traced. An annotated list of characters supplies brief information on the chief characters in the work.

A selection of critical extracts, derived from previously published material by leading critics, then follows. The extracts consist of such things as statements by the author on his work, early reviews of the work, and later evaluations down to the present day. The items are arranged chronologically by date of first publication. A bibliography of Milton's writings (including a complete listing of all books he wrote, cowrote, edited, and translated, and selected posthumous publications), a list of additional books and articles on him and on *Paradise Lost,* and an index of themes and ideas conclude the volume.

Harold Bloom is Sterling Professor of the Humanities at Yale University and Henry W. and Albert A. Berg Professor of English at the New York University Graduate School. He is the author of twenty books and the editor of more than thirty anthologies of literature and literary criticism.

Professor Bloom's works include *Shelley's Mythmaking* (1959), *The Visionary Company* (1961), *Blake's Apocalypse* (1963), *Yeats* (1970), *A Map of Misreading* (1975), *Kabbalah and Criticism* (1975), and *Agon: Towards a Theory of Revisionism* (1982). *The Anxiety of Influence* (1973) sets forth Professor Bloom's provocative theory of the literary relationships between the great writers and their predecessors. His most recent books are *The American Religion* (1992) and *The Western Canon* (1994).

Professor Bloom earned his Ph.D. from Yale University in 1955 and has served on the Yale faculty since then. He is a 1985 MacArthur Foundation Award recipient and served as the Charles Eliot Norton Professor of Poetry at Harvard University in 1987–88. He is currently the editor of the Chelsea House series Major Literary Characters and Modern Critical Views, and other Chelsea House series in literary criticism.

Introduction

HAROLD BLOOM

John Milton intended his epic poem, *Paradise Lost,* to be a theodicy, justifying the ways of God to men and women. That was not, however, his entire purpose in writing the last European epic to challenge Homer, Vergil, and Dante. The challenge, on Milton's part, was overt: His poem asserts that it will achieve things unattempted yet in prose or rhyme, which implies that even the Bible and Shakespeare are to be surpassed, in some aspects anyway. No one would grant Milton's Satan a darker sublimity than that of the Shakespearean hero-villains who deeply influenced *Paradise Lost*'s fallen angel: Iago, Macbeth, Edmund in *King Lear.* It could be argued, though, that the Miltonic account of the Creation in book seven transcends its prime source, the first chapter of Genesis. Shelley slyly observed that "the Devil owes everything to Milton," since our versions of Satan before *Paradise Lost* are sparse and uninteresting compared to Milton's Shakespearean Satan. T. S. Eliot, in his anti-Miltonic phase, dismissed the protagonist of *Paradise Lost* as "Milton's curly haired, Byronic hero," but that was the same T. S. Eliot who assured us that *Hamlet* was certainly an aesthetic failure and who dismissed Emerson's *Essays* as "already an encumbrance." Satan's hair can be debated, if you are into that sort of thing, but Lord Byron's Cain and Manfred are not very Satanic.

William Blake's famous jest, that Milton was "a true poet and of the Devil's party without knowing it," is a more imaginative suggestion than most critics have taken it to be. There are two Satans in the poem, and the great one abandons us after his marvelous speech atop Mount Niphates (book four, 33–113). His debased form undergoes continuous further degradation until it ends as "a monstrous serpent on his belly prone" in book ten. The Milton who torments Satan is certainly not of the Devil's party, but he is also more of a theologian than he is a true poet. The poem's true puzzle is not Satan, but Milton's God, who is personal yet not a person, and aesthetically is greatly inferior to the Satan of books one through four. Messiah, in the poem, is also an aesthetic, and indeed a spiritual disaster. Are we to be content with Jesus Christ as a heavenly Rommel or Patton, victoriously leading the armored attack upon the rebel army, riding as he does in the Chariot of Paternal Deity?

Satan, *in the poem,* simply is a much better poet than God and Messiah are, which cannot have been Milton's intention. We have the problem then of why Milton invested so much of his poetic power in Satan, and so little in the irascible, mean-spirited, sanctimonious God of the poem. I think one answer is that John Milton's actual God is not identical with the character that *Paradise Lost* calls God. The true God of the poem pragmatically is the voice that narrates it, a voice that fuses spirit and power. Milton had such confidence in that voice that he enables it to speak as the prior revelation, as the truth of the origins that preceded even the truth of the Five Books of Moses. Milton uses the word "first" five times in *Paradise Lost's* first twenty-eight lines, and by "first" he meant "earliest." Compared to his own poem, Milton sees not only the *Iliad,* the *Aeneid,* and *The Divine Comedy* as belated works, but the Bible as well. The author of *Paradise Lost* sees things earliest, which is to see them as they truly were. We ought never to forget that Milton was a Christian heretic, rather than a Calvinist. He was a sect of one, and all of his heresies fused in his monism, his refusal to accept the Pauline dualism of the split between flesh and spirit.

Milton did not believe in the Trinity or in a creation out of nothingness, and though he believed in the Resurrection, he was a Mortalist and so held that the soul and the body die together and in the fullness of time would be resurrected together. His blindness only caused Milton to exalt all of the senses even more fiercely. My favorite Milton critic, W. B. C. Watkins, first emphasized the extent to which Milton was a monist and a poet of the senses:

> We cannot overstress a fundamental truth about Milton which we find endlessly proliferated in his work. At his most creative, he accepts the whole range from the physical, specifically the senses, to the ultimate Divine as *absolutely unbroken.* This glad acceptance means that he is free to speak of any order of being (extending to inanimate matter) in identical sensuous terms as the great common denominator.

This means that, for Milton, the highest reaches of the spiritual could be apprehended by the human senses, which pragmatically Milton refused to regard as being fallen. That is why Milton's angels have bodies, however subtle, and enjoy a sexual life, one that appears to be more strenuously complete than our own. By refusing to distinguish between spiritual power and natural energies, Milton created the dilemma for himself: In what sense are we fallen men and women? The Puritans maintained that God's grace worked to abolish the natural man, but Milton was no Puritan. For him, the function of grace was to perfect us, to aid in our regeneration, but never to negate our humanity.

Milton never used the words "dualism" or "dualist," because they did not come into use until the early eighteenth century and so were not available to him. But he incarnated dualism in his Satan, particularly in the dark meditation of Satan atop Mount Niphates at the start of book four of *Paradise Lost*. For Satan, spirit and matter have separated, and he is a ruined soul trapped in the body of death. Whereas Milton refused to see reason and passion as being in conflict, they clash endlessly in the tormented Satan. It is, paradoxically, the strength of his passion that makes Satan the great aesthetic success of the poem, but then Milton is one of the most passionate of all poets, ever. Miltonic monism itself is a passion, rather than a philosophy. Passion or pathos, as we sometimes forget, is primal for Milton, who reminds us that poetry must be both passionate and sensuous. The tragic Satan of *Paradise Lost* is the lasting triumph of Milton's own passion for poetry. ❖

Biography of
John Milton

John Milton was born to a Puritan family in London on December 9, 1608. His father was a successful scrivener (a copyist in a law office) and an amateur musician. Milton inherited his father's creative abilities rather than his business acumen and was encouraged in his intellectual endeavors.

Milton received an excellent education, beginning with tutoring by Puritan scholar and minister Thomas Young. While at St. Paul's School, he studied everything from astronomy to history and rhetoric to Italian and Hebrew. Possessing a voracious appetite for knowledge, the young boy would stay up till midnight reading and writing.

In 1625, Milton enrolled in Christ's College, Cambridge. After a disagreement with his first tutor there, he transferred to another teacher and settled into a rigorous course of study. As a result of his studious and prudish manner, Milton was nicknamed "The Lady of Christ's" by fellow students. The serious student was especially influenced by Latin, English, and Italian poets, such as Ovid, Ben Jonson, and Giovanni della Casa. He exhibited skill in crafting his own Latin elegies and declared an intention to compose an English epic on some serious theme. His most notable work during this early stage of development was the English ode "On the Morning of Christ's Nativity," written in late 1629.

Besides exploring literature, Milton gained exposure to the religious controversies being discussed at the university. He sided with the Puritans in their arguments against the Anglicans. In particular, he opposed the demand for conformity among the clergy imposed by Archbishop of Canterbury William Laud. Unwilling to take Anglican orders, he gave up the pursuit of an ecclesiastical career and returned to his father's home in Horton after receiving his master's degree in 1632.

Milton continued his education on his own in Horton. In addition to studying religious issues and reading classical texts, he examined history from the Roman Empire to modern times.

Around 1632 he wrote the companion lyrics "L'Allegro" and "Il Penseroso." In 1634 he composed the masterful masque *Comus* for performance at the earl of Bridgewater's inauguration; when it was issued three years later, it became Milton's first published book. This semidramatic poem evidences Milton's religious nature, focusing on how "the Lady" protects her chastity from temptation. The death of a college friend inspired his other acclaimed work from this period, "Lycidas" (1637), a pastoral elegy that criticizes the corrupt clergy and meditates upon fate and immortality.

After six years of independent scholarship, Milton embarked in 1637 upon a European tour. For almost two years he visited Paris, Florence, Rome, Naples, and Geneva. He traveled in distinguished intellectual circles, meeting such notables as Galileo and the Dutch statesman Hugo Grotius, and composed a few Latin poems. When he heard news of political turmoil in England, he cut short his trip and returned home in 1639.

Although it was around this time that Milton developed an interest in writing an epic about the fall of humankind, politics drew his attention away from poetry. While running a small private school in London, he published five tracts in 1641 and 1642 that vigorously opposed the Anglican bishops and advocated Presbyterianism. His prose contained flashes of brilliant writing but generally was uneven in quality.

Another subject soon roused Milton's pamphlet-writing passion. In 1642 at the age of thirty-three, he married sixteen-year-old Royalist Mary Powell. After a month, Mrs. Milton left to visit her parents and did not return. Angry at this abandonment, Milton published *The Doctrine and Discipline of Divorce* (1643), arguing that incompatibility was just grounds for divorce. Milton's three subsequent pamphlets on the subject drew upon Scripture to bolster his case. His prodivorce campaign marked him as an independent and earned him notoriety. In 1644 he published his most eloquent pamphlet, *Areopagitica,* which opposed a statute that would restrict the freedom of the press.

Milton entered a more domestic phase in 1645, when he was reconciled with his wife. In 1646, his wife's family, ruined by the Civil War, briefly joined the Milton household, and his daughters Anne and Mary were born in 1646 and 1648. After his father's death in 1647, Milton left his school and moved to a smaller house. A collection of his poems was published in 1645, and he otherwise occupied his time researching *The History of Britain* (published in 1670).

The 1649 trial of Charles I spurred Milton to reenter the public realm. He wrote *The Tenure of Kings and Magistrates* to argue that monarchs could not rule without their subjects' consent. After Charles I's execution, Milton was appointed secretary for foreign languages to the council of state, where he handled public relations as well as foreign correspondence and translation duties. Although his eyesight was failing, he resolutely undertook the defense of Charles's execution and the new regime, starting with *Eikonoklastes* (1649) and continuing with three ferocious Latin defenses.

Besides the political upheaval, a series of personal crises took its toll on Milton in the 1650s. In 1652 he became completely blind and required numerous assistants to continue his work. Later that year his only son died and his wife perished while giving birth to a third daughter, Deborah. In 1656 he married Katharine Woodcock, but less than two years later she and their child died. Oliver Cromwell died in 1658, leaving England vulnerable to the monarchy's return. Milton held firm to his beliefs and boldly published three pamphlets advocating a republican government, religious liberty, and an unpaid clergy. When Charles II assumed the throne in 1660, Milton was briefly imprisoned and was financially ruined.

Despite his misfortunes, Milton remained devoutly religious and resumed work on his poetry. In 1663 he married Elizabeth Minshull and enjoyed a happy family life with her, despite becoming alienated from his two eldest daughters. He completed his masterpiece, *Paradise Lost,* an epic of creation and the fall of mankind, in 1665 and received critical acclaim upon its publication in 1667. In 1671 he published *Paradise Regain'd,* a short epic that reflects upon Christ's victory over Satan's temptations, and *Samson Agonistes,* a poetic drama about the biblical hero. Still energetic in his final years, he produced *The History of Britain,* a treatise on logic, an anti-Catholic pamphlet, an English grammar, a collection of his Latin correspondence, a second edition of his poems, a second edition of *Paradise Lost,* and the theological treatise *De Doctrina Christiana* (Of Christian doctrine; not published until 1825). Suffering from gout, Milton died on November 8, 1674. Today he remains one of the towering figures in English literature. ❖

Thematic and Structural Analysis

John Milton fused his poetic genius with his staunch Protestant theology and vast literary knowledge to create the great epic, *Paradise Lost*. He drew extensively on classical mythology, Homer and Vergil, Christian Scripture and theology, and British political events of his own time to fashion a sweeping narrative that vivifies his conception of humanity's relationship with the Divine. Milton's poem does more than retell the story of the Fall as it is recorded in Genesis. He supplies a concrete narrative to explicate abstract theological and psychological ideas, while criticizing seventeenth-century British religious, political, and scientific beliefs.

The poem is written in blank verse (without rhyme). In its second edition (1674), Milton, at the request of readers, added arguments, or plot summaries, at the opening of each book. Milton's use of Scripture reflects an interpretation prevalent in his time: Old Testament characters and events prefigure those of the New Testament.

The first edition of *Paradise Lost* (1667) was divided into ten books; in later editions these were divided into twelve books. The poem began as a drama, which may account for the striking soliloquies found in the poem's best scenes. Perhaps Milton's piety kept him from fully animating his representations of God and the Son; most of their speeches fall flat when compared to passages spoken by Satan. In his attempt to "justify the ways of God to men," Milton created in Satan one of the most engaging and complex characters of English literature and established the standard conception of Satan for Western Christendom.

The argument of **book one** tells us that this book proposes the "whole subject": humanity's disobedience and the loss of Paradise. The poem begins with a traditional invocation: a call upon the Heavenly Muse to aid the poet in accomplishing a work "unattempted yet in prose or rhyme." Milton writes that his purpose is to "assert Eternal Providence." He asks what caused our "Grand Parents" to revolt against God, and the answer, "the infernal Serpent," is given. The rebellion of Lucifer—once chief of the angels and now called Satan—and his loyal angels is described briefly.

The action begins with the rebel angels awakening, confused and vanquished, in the "fiery gulf" of Hell. Satan's next-in-power, Be'lzebub, speaks first and marks the striking change in Satan's appearance: "into what pit thou seest / From what height fallen." What Be'lzebub articulates as a change in appearance from "transcendent brightness" to fallen gloom Satan reveals as a determined change in vision as well:

> Fall'n Cherub, to be weak is miserable,
> Doing or suffering: but of this be sure—
> To do aught good never will be our task,
> But ever to do ill our sole delight,
> As being the contrary to his high will
> Whom we resist.

Satan surveys his slumbering army, which Milton identifies as the earliest incarnations of later mythological gods. Satan embraces his new position in a passage important for its psychological as well as theological arguments:

> The mind is its own place, and in itself
> Can make a Heaven of Hell, a Hell of Heaven.
> What matter where, if I be still the same,
> And what I should be, all but less than he
> Whom thunder hath made greater? Here at least
> We shall be free; th' Almighty hath not built
> Here for his envy, will not drive us hence:
> Here we may reign secure; and, in my choice,
> To reign is worth ambition, though in Hell:
> Better to reign in Hell than serve in Heaven.

Satan comforts his forces by maintaining that they may still retake Heaven, and he further mentions that a new world and a new creature are shortly to be created in Heaven. He then rouses his troops, who raise a great palace, Pandemonium, by sorcery and assemble there to plot their next course of action.

In **book two** Satan sits on a grand throne—described with echoes of Spenser's depiction of Pride in *The Faerie Queene*—and calls for debate on the best plan to reclaim Heaven.

Moloch, sceptered king and fiercest warrior, advises direct attack. Belial, more reasonable, warns that more war could result in greater torments if they fail. Mammon ("money" or "wealth") points out how even a return to their former state in Heaven would be unacceptable: They should carve their own kingdom in Hell and reign there. Each of these proposals represents a different course of disobedience to which humankind falls prey in its relation to God: overt rebellion, insincere submission, and idolatry.

Be'lzebub points out that Hell was given to them not as a safe retreat but as an eternal dungeon. He reminds them of the prophetic story in Heaven of another world inhabited by man, "less in power and excellence" than the angels. He proposes that a scout be chosen to determine the vulnerability of man.

Satan praises their debate and appoints himself the scout. He undertakes the long journey, finally reaching the outer gates of Hell. The locked gates are guarded by a monstrous being, Death, and his mother, Sin, who safeguards the keys. Sin reveals the pair's true identities to Satan, who has failed to recognize them: Sin is his daughter, sprung from his head as he plotted against God, and Death is their son. Sin unlocks the gates and is unable to shut them behind Satan, making possible humankind's later descent. With the aid of Chaos, Satan is led to the outermost reaches of the universe. The closer he gets to Earth's system, the easier his passage becomes.

In **book three** Milton exemplifies two crucial tenets of Christian—particularly Protestant—theology: man's free will and God's grace and divine justice. That God himself speaks of predestination, or the preselection of those to be saved, adds force to the doctrine. Milton also explicates the rationale for the Atonement, or the sacrifice of the Son of God in exchange for man's redemption. Milton makes clear that although God foresees man's disobedience, he does not bring about its occurrence or in any way interfere with man's free will.

To the Son, God foretells Satan's success in perverting man. Satan and his followers are more guilty than man for transgressing on their own, without a tempter, and God states that he is inclined to show man mercy because he was led astray. The Son encourages his Father to extend his grace to man, and

God agrees, with the stipulation that justice must also be satisfied. In the future, those who are predestined for salvation will hear God's call and repent. However, man has committed high treason against the Godhead, and he and his progeny must die, unless someone of sufficient charity dies in man's place. The Son, alone capable of so great a love, volunteers to do so.

God proclaims that the Son must join his nature with man's nature and that he will be born of a virgin and die:

> Thou, therefore, whom thou only canst redeem,
> Their nature also to thy nature join;
> And be thyself Man among men on Earth,
> Made flesh, when time shall be, of virgin seed,
> By wondrous birth; be thou in Adam's room
> The head of all Mankind, though Adam's son.

God proclaims that as both man and God, the Son will reign, exalted above all others; and at God's decree the multitude of Heaven shows homage to the Son.

Satan lands on the outermost orb of the universe. He wanders into the Limbo of Vanity, which consists of various false beliefs and superstitions, primarily the customs of several Catholic orders and of the papacy. Satan then ascends toward Heaven and the Sun and encounters the angel Uriel. Satan disguises himself as a lesser angel, zealous to defend man, and manages to learn man's dwelling place from Uriel.

In **book four** Milton describes Satan's confused emotional state as he approaches Eden as "much revolving." In some of the most powerful verses of the poem, Satan's own words reveal his turmoil:

> O Sun, to tell thee how I hate thy beams,
> That bring to my remembrance from what state
> I fell, how glorious once above thy sphere,
> Till pride and worse ambition threw me down,
> Warring in Heaven against Heaven's matchless King:
> . . . .
> Me miserable! which way shall I fly
> Infinite wrath and infinite despair?
> Which way I fly is Hell; myself am Hell;
> And, in the lowest deep, a lower deep
> Still threatening to devour me opens wide,
> To which the Hell I suffer seems a Heaven.

Satan suffers more during his attempt to defraud man than he did imprisoned in Hell. His psychological state is emblematic of the fallen human condition.

Still, Satan refuses to submit to God's will and leaps over the fence into Eden. Milton describes Satan as the "first grand Thief," thereby contrasting him with the Son of God. In a representative echo, Milton borrows from the Gospel of John, in which Jesus says, "He that entereth not by the door into the sheepfold, but climbeth up some other way, the same is a thief and a robber."

Satan flies into the Tree of Life, and, disguised as a cormorant, observes Adam and Eve. Milton reaffirms the distinctiveness of the sexes and of the ordained patriarchal order:

> For contemplation he and valour formed,
> For softness she and sweet attractive grace;
> He for God only, she for God in him.

"With grief," Milton writes, Satan admires their beauty and their only slight inferiority to heavenly beings, but his intent remains unchanged:

> Hell shall unfold,
> To entertain you two, her widest gates,
> And send forth all her kings; there will be room,
> Not like these narrow limits, to receive
> Your numerous offspring. . . .

The metaphorical comparison of the narrow gate of salvation to the wide gates of Hell appears in the Gospels of both Luke and Matthew.

Satan overhears Adam and Eve talking of their reverence for God and of their devotion to one another. Adam unwittingly reveals God's command, under penalty of death—a concept unknown to him—not to eat from the Tree of Knowledge. Meanwhile, Uriel warns Gabriel of Satan's presence, and Gabriel vows to find Satan before morning. Milton uses the next scene—Adam and Eve worshipping God before sleep—to praise both worship free from excessive rites, in keeping with his Protestant beliefs, and to defend wedded physical love as ordained by God.

Gabriel, along with other angels in his command, searches for Satan. He is found crouched by Eve's ear and speaking to her while she sleeps. Led by a heavenly sign, Gabriel allows Satan to flee Eden.

Upon awakening, in **book five**, Eve tells Adam of her troubling dream: An angel bid her to eat the fruit of the forbidden tree. After doing so, she was able to fly up to Heaven. Adam is disturbed and comforts her. He explains that the chief faculty, Reason, retreats during sleep, and Fancy takes over. She may dream, then, what she would never consent to do while awake. Cheered, they proceed to their morning prayer.

God sends Raphael, "the sociable Spirit," to remind Adam of his happy state and of his free will and to enjoin him not to swerve from the path of obedience. Furthermore, Raphael is told to warn Adam of the threat unloosed from Hell and to convey to him the circumstances of Satan's rebellion and fall.

We learn that Satan, formerly Lucifer, was enraged with jealousy at the ascension of the Son to God's throne. He lured one-third of Heaven's angels to follow him under the guise of preparing a grand display of adoration for the Son. Once they arrived at the far north of Heaven, Satan convinced all those angels present to rebel with him, save one: Abdiel would not follow and denounced him. Abdiel is possibly a stand-in for Milton, who saw himself as single-handedly defending the pure tenets of the faith:

> So spake the Seraph Abdiel, faithful found;
> Among the faithless, faithful only he;
> Among innumerable false unmoved,
> Unshaken, unseduced, unterrified,
> His loyalty he kept, his love, his zeal;
> Nor number nor example with him wrought
> To swerve from truth, or change his constant mind. . . .

In **book six** Raphael continues telling Adam about the fall of Lucifer, and the battles of the angels' rebellion. Abdiel, having survived one night among the rebel angels, returns a hero and is addressed by the Sovereign Voice:

> The easier conquest now
> Remains thee, aided by this host of friends,

Back on thy foes more glorious to return
Than scorned thou didst depart; and to subdue
By force who reason for their law refuse—
Right reason for their law, and for their King
Messiah, who by right of merit reigns.

Throughout book six Milton recreates seventeenth-century concerns with reason, truth, war, and royal sovereignty. The army of Gabriel and Michael is arrayed with reason, force of nature, truth, and order. Abdiel and Satan exchange views on liberty, free will, and servitude. Invoking God and Nature, Abdiel strikes Satan with his sword. Satan falls back ten paces, signaling the opening of the battle.

The battle rages through the northern section of Heaven and hangs in the balance for another day, until Michael cuts Satan—his first experience of pain. Gabriel fights other rebel angels in another section of Heaven. Though the battle rages for three days, the angels of Heaven have

[s]uch high advantages their innocence
Gave them above their foes—not to have sinned,
Not to have disobeyed; in fight they stood
Unwearied, unobnoxious to be pained
By wound. . . .

Satan calls a council, and Nisroch, one of his followers, explains that fighting in pain from sin has put Satan's legions at a disadvantage. Satan replies that the beauty of Heaven springs from the dark power underneath, which they can harness for their warfare. Encouraged, Satan's angels return to the fight. The following days' battles include Satan's cannons, made from trees—nature defiled. God's angels are empowered to respond by tearing up the landscape of Heaven: Nature, in God's power, overcomes Satan's army.

God calls the Son to end the battle. On the dawn of the third day, the chariot of the Son, drawn by the powers of Heaven in the shape of four stars, blazes forth to drive Satan and his army into the abyss of Hell. For nine days they fall. Heaven is restored to natural order, and the Son returns to a celebration. Raphael ends his narration by pointing out that the events of

Heaven are mirrored on Earth and so Satan will try to overcome Adam as well.

In **book seven** Adam, amazed by the battles of Heaven, asks Raphael how Earth was formed, acknowledging that his understanding of godly matters is imperfect. Raphael agrees to answer, also conceding that Adam's understanding need not go beyond a certain scope:

> But Knowledge is as food, and needs no less
> Her temperance over appetite, to know
> In measure what the mind may well contain;
> Oppresses else with surfeit, and soon turns
> Wisdom to folly, as nourishment to wind.

First, Raphael tells of God's decision to create a world between Heaven and Hell, where a new type of being would dwell. The new beings would have free will that they would use to earn their way back to Heaven. God sent the Son to do the work of creation, which progressed according to the scheme of Genesis. Milton elaborates on the biblical images, ending with the creation of beings who stood erect and possessed the "sanctity of Reason." His work finished, the Creator returned to Heaven amid great rejoicing. Milton ends book seven with praise for the creation of the heavens, for the power of God, and for the creation of man.

Book eight addresses a core theme of *Paradise Lost:* the proper place of reason and knowledge and their balanced relation to faith, truth, and trust. Adam admits his thirst for knowledge and his imperfect understanding. He thanks Raphael for satisfying his questions—but he has another query: How has Nature ordered the celestial bodies? Milton tells us that queenlike Eve lingers nearby, listening though not understanding, admired by all that surrounds her.

Raphael does not fault Adam's curiosity but lectures him on astronomy, discussing the subject as it was understood in the mid-seventeenth century. Milton, via Raphael, allows for the scientific discoveries of the movement of Earth and the planets and even the existence of many other "suns," but Heaven is far out of both man's sight and understanding and is designed to remain so. Adam should not trouble himself with distant details. Adam agrees, claiming to be quite satisfied with Raphael's explanation of astronomy:

> That not to know at large of things remote
> From use, obscure and subtle, but to know
> That which before us lies in daily life,
> Is the prime wisdom. . . .

Adam then invites Raphael to hear his own story, his memories of waking from his creation. Raphael agrees, since he was guarding the gates of Hell and was not present during Creation. Adam relates his awe at his surroundings, his waking gaze Heavenward. He tells of how he surveyed himself, gained speech, and then began naming the features of the landscape. He wondered at his own creation, sat drowsily, and then perceived a divine being, who escorted him through Paradise and to the Supreme Creator. Adam was addressed by God, who sternly warned him against the Tree of Knowledge. Then, in softer tones, God commended the Earth and all its residents to Adam's care, bidding him to name them and respect their natures. But Adam was not yet satisfied: He wanted a mate, as other creatures had.

Milton uses the discussion between God and Adam to argue against the priesthood—against any being striving to emulate God's solitary state. God congratulated Adam on knowing his place and agreed to create a mate for him. While Adam slept, Eve was created from his rib. He awoke to her presence, over-joyed and thankful to God for granting his wish so perfectly. In virgin modesty, she was led to the nuptial bower.

The book concludes with Adam expressing his infinite love for Eve, and Raphael warning Adam of love's proper boundaries. Reason and nature are again invoked, Raphael reminding Adam of the tests of free will and temptation. With Adam's thanks, the two part company.

Milton introduces the subject of **book nine**, the Fall of Man, by invoking ancient mythologies and chivalric storytelling, but insists that Heaven's influence is urging the story onward. Satan, having surveyed Earth for seven nights, rides the Tigris

River underground, surfacing with it in the morning mist at the Tree of Life in Eden. In Eden he searches for the serpent, finding it the "subtlest" of all the beasts, and inhabits its body. Satan bemoans the beauty of the world, noting, "For only in destroying I find ease / To my relentless thoughts." Although aware of revenge's meager part, he resolves that "spite then with spite is best repaid."

Adam and Eve begin their day by tending the garden, walking, and talking. Their discussion amounts to a debate on the Protestant work ethic. Eve suggests that they work separately, and they discuss marital expectation, commitment, trust, order, and protection. They have been warned of Satan's intent, and the weaker Eve argues (using reason, which Milton suddenly feminizes) for her own free will, which Adam in his love grants her, as God has granted it to him. Adam notes that reason can also be deceived.

The serpent espies Eve, "fairest unsupported flower," and is first disarmed and then further enraged by what he will never truly possess. He draws Eve's attention and speaks flatteringly to her. Surprised, Eve asks how he came to speak. The serpent explains that the Tree of Knowledge gave him human powers and can therefore render Adam and Eve godlike.

At Eve's request they find the Tree, and Eve recognizes it, declaring it forbidden to her. The serpent argues that she will attain wisdom, and Eve notes that the serpent has not died, as God had promised. She eats greedily, then drunkenly praises the Tree, musing on her choice and aware that she has parted from Adam.

Adam and Eve meet near the Tree, she with a bough in her hand and Adam appalled at what she has done. Eve tells Adam the "true" nature of the Tree, and Adam, forlorn at her mistake, resolves to die with her. He reasons that God will not entirely forsake them. Again, Milton focuses their discussion on the rights and duties of marriage in the fallen state.

Adam eats. Inebriated, he claims that she has never looked so lovely, and they indulge in amorous play, fall asleep afterwards, and wake up to the horror of their nakedness and their mistake. Adam chastises Eve, and they cover their nakedness, then sit down to cry. They argue, Adam pointing out his mistake in "overtrusting."

In **book ten** the guardian angels of Earth return to Heaven, but God tells them not to blame themselves for Satan's entrance, because all was foretold. Justice and mercy will prevail by way of the Son's intercession.

God sends the Son to Earth and shames Adam for his transgression; Eve blames the serpent, and God curses Satan through the serpent. God proclaims that Eve will suffer childbirth and be subject to man's will; Adam will suffer and toil for his keep and will die.

Meanwhile, Sin and Death have been waiting for Satan's return at Hell's gate and, feeling "new strength arise," decide that Satan has been successful. They begin constructing a wide road, a bridge across Chaos, for the future commerce between Earth and Hell. They meet Satan, who left Earth on perceiving the arrival of the Son. The three rejoice at their new opportunities on Earth, and Satan continues on to Hell.

Milton describes Hell much like a royal court. Satan lectures Hell's inhabitants about his colonization of the "New World." His listeners turn to serpents. A grove of fruiting trees, Trees of Knowledge, spring up, which in their hunger the hissing and writhing monsters try to climb, but to no avail: Their mouths fill with ashes.

Meanwhile, Sin and Death take up their work in Paradise. God watches and notes that they may think he has abandoned Earth, but indeed all is part of the plan that his Son will bring to resolution. God charges his angels to inflict Earth with inclement weather and odd planetary motions:

> Thus began
> Outrage from lifeless things; but Discord first,
> Daughter of Sin, among th' irrational
> Death introduced through fierce antipathy:
> Beast now with beast, 'gan war, and fowl with fowl . . .
> nor stood much in awe
> Of Man, but fled him. . . .

Adam bemoans the change and wishes the punishment to affect only him, so that others may enjoy Paradise. He finds death a mockery, since the spirit lives on, and wonders at the depth of God's wrath for creating such a system: "In me all / Posterity stand cursed." He finds no way out of this consciousness. He laments, sees Eve, calls her "Serpent," and wonders why God, who peopled Heaven with only masculine angels, created such a "fair defect of nature."

Eve begs him not to forsake her. The serpent tricked her, and, losing both man and God, she has the worst portion and wishes to take the sole blame. Adam has pity, and they discuss how they will carry on. Eve suggests that they should not reproduce, but end humanity with their own deaths, possibly through suicide. Adam replies that God has a plan, which they should follow; the Son of God is to be their redeemer, and so they will have to people the Earth for this divine purpose. He goes on to explain how humanity will try to master the conditions of Earth, prostrate themselves, and revere God—which they begin doing.

In **book eleven** the Son pleads with God to hear Adam and Eve's prayers and to yield them "to better life" after their deaths. God assents, but decrees that they must leave Paradise before they eat from the Tree of Life:

> I at first with two fair gifts
> Created him endowed—with Happiness
> And Immortality; that fondly lost,
> This other served but to eternize woe,
> Till I provided Death: so Death becomes
> His final remedy. . . .

God sends Michael and a group of "flaming warriors" to drive the "sinful pair" from Paradise, but the archangel is instructed to console Adam with "what shall come in future days."

Meanwhile, Adam feels that his prayers have been heard, and he and Eve assume that they have been spared death and are free to live, if in a fallen state, in Paradise. Adam perceives the descent of a heavenly being, whom he goes out to greet. Michael, in human form and clad in military garb, informs him of God's decree. Adam grieves but submits, and Eve, unseen but listening, laments. Michael assures them that God is present everywhere on Earth, and all Earth was created for them.

Michael bids Eve to sleep while he leads Adam up the highest hill in Paradise to behold God's vision. Milton explains the contrast between this scene and Satan's tempting of Christ in the desert. Michael reveals to Adam the murder of Abel by Cain and shows him other means of death; namely, by disease. Adam is told he may avoid painful death by temperance and thereby reach old age. Adam is shown the wicked progeny of Cain and the faithful line of his third son, Seth. Adam is also shown the Sons of God begetting giants on Earth and the gradual dissolution of man's relationship with God. When Adam despairs that the race will end, Michael shows him the righteous Noah and his ark, the Flood, and the rainbow's marking of a new covenant with God. To Adam's questioning, Michael assures him that God will never again destroy the Earth by flood.

In **book twelve** Milton continues Michael's narrative, relating the events after the Flood. His reimagined biblical stories contrast faith and disobedience. Michael depicts the rise of Nimrod's kingdom and the confusing of tongues at the Tower of Babel, and Milton uses the occasion to raise issues of religious and civil freedom: "human left from human free."

Michael introduces "faithful Abraham" and his lineage of servants also faithful to God: Isaac, Jacob (Israel), and Joseph. He relates Moses' leading of the Israelites from Egypt and the people's deliverance into the Promised Land.

Adam questions the necessity of the law; Michael answers with a "faith, not works" argument, a crucial Protestant formulation that faith, not obedience to the law, is the ultimate good. The law can help man avoid sin but cannot expiate it; Michael tells Adam, "Some more precious blood must be paid for man" (as opposed to the animal sacrifices commanded by Jewish law).

Underscoring Milton's typological view of Scripture, Michael speaks of "a better cov'nant, disciplined / From shadowy types to truth." He describes Christ's place in David's lineage and the circumstances of his birth: his virgin mother and "[h]is sire /

The Power of the Most High." Adam, believing an actual fight between the serpent and Christ will take place, asks where and when the battle will happen. Michael, explaining the Crucifixion, repeatedly emphasizes Christ's obedience, his fulfillment of the law, and his acceptance of Man's penalty:

> By faith not void of works. This godlike act
> Annuls thy doom, the death thou shouldst have died,
> In sin for ever lost from life; this act
> Shall bruise the head of Satan, crush his strength,
> Defeating Sin and Death, his two main arms,
> And fix far deeper in his head their stings
> Than temporal death shall bruise the Victor's heel. . . .

Instructed and reassured, Adam departs to wake Eve, who has been asleep and dreaming comforting dreams: "For God is also in sleep, and dreams advise." With blazing sword ahead, Michael leads the couple by the hands to the eastern gate of Paradise:

> Some natural tears they dropped, but wiped them soon;
> The world was all before them, where to choose
> Their place of rest, and Providence their guide:
> They hand in hand, with wandering steps and slow,
> Through Eden took their solitary way. ❖

—Martha Serpas

List of Characters

Satan, called *Lucifer,* or "light-bearer," before he is driven from Heaven, is the fallen chief of the angels. In his envy of the Son of God, Satan, whose name means "adversary," leads a rebellion against Heaven and is thrown into Hell. He corrupts God's new creation, Earth, by tempting Adam and Eve to sin. In parts of the text, *Serpent* is another name for Satan, who takes over the creature's body while it sleeps. Disguised as the serpent, Satan tricks Eve into eating from the Tree of Knowledge. God curses the serpent for this evil act.

Adam is God's creature, made superior to all inhabitants of Earth and only slightly inferior to the heavenly beings. He is the vehicle of Milton's thinking on many issues: faith, trust, love, honor, marriage, and obedience.

Eve is Adam's partner, created from his rib. She is beautiful and weak and is tempted by Satan. Her actions result in the Fall of Man.

Raphael is the "Sociable Spirit," sent by God to strengthen Adam's faith and to warn him of Satan's approach. Raphael relates to Adam the great battle in Heaven, Satan's fall, and the story of the Creation.

Michael is an archangel who fights against the rebel angels. He is chosen to lead Adam and Eve out of the garden and to show Adam man's future on Earth.

Abdiel is the only one of Lucifer's angels who refuses to go along with the rebellion and is heralded as a hero. He may also represent Milton, as the sole defender of true faith.

Gabriel is chief of the angelic guards. He greets Eve as the mother of mankind in words similar to those in the Gospel of Luke, in which Gabriel informs Mary that she will bear the Son of God. Gabriel casts Satan out of Paradise.

Uriel is an angel, the regent of the orb of the Sun. He reveals to Satan man's dwelling place in Paradise and then warns Gabriel of Satan's approach.

Be'lzebub is one of the rebel angels and next to Satan in power. The name means "lord of the flies." Satan follows Be'lzebub's counsel when he decides to tempt man on Earth.

Belial ("wickedness") is one of Satan's fallen angels, whom Milton describes as a "lewd" spirit. Belial argues against immediate war and for what Milton calls "peaceful sloth." Milton invokes the stories of Sodom (Genesis 19) and of Gibeah (Judges 19) in which rape is threatened or committed by "the sons of Belial."

Mammon is one of Satan's fallen angels, who speaks in favor of ruling Hell and not plotting to regain Heaven. He represents the idolatrous replacement of God.

Moloch ("king") is one of Satan's fallen angels. He urges Satan to continue an all-out war against Heaven. Milton draws from several histories and mythologies concerning "the strongest and fiercest spirit," including the narrative in First Kings, in which Moloch, a false god, is worshipped by Solomon.

Sin is Satan's daughter, sprung from his head. She guards the gates of Hell and, after the Fall of Man, builds the road to Earth with her son, Death.

Death is Sin's son by Satan, an incestuous progeny. He guards the gates of Hell with his mother and helps build the road from Hell to Earth. Death works first on the plants and animals of Paradise. ✤

Critical Views

[John Dryden (1631–1700), the greatest English poet of the later seventeenth century, was well acquainted with Milton during the final years of the latter's life. In this extract, however, Dryden—who was also one of the pioneers of English literary criticism—takes Milton to task on his long passages of philosophical exposition, his use of archaic language, and his decision to abandon rhyme for blank verse in *Paradise Lost.*]

As for Mr. *Milton,* whom we all admire with so much Justice, his Subject is not that of an Heroique Poem; properly so call'd: His Design is the Losing of our Happiness; his Event is not prosperous, like that of all other Epique Works: His Heavenly Machines are many, and his Humane Persons are but two. But I will not take Mr. ⟨Thomas⟩ *Rymer's* Work out of his Hands. He has promis'd the World a Critique on that Author; wherein, tho' he will not allow his Poem for Heroick, I hope he will grant us, that his Thoughts are elevated, his Words Sounding, and that no Man has so happily Copy'd the Manner of *Homer;* or so copiously translated his *Grecisms,* and the *Latin* Elegancies of *Virgil.* 'Tis true, he runs into a flat of Thought, sometimes for a Hundred Lines together, but 'tis when he is got into a Track of Scripture: His Antiquated words were his Choice, not his Necessity; for therein he imitated *Spencer,* as *Spencer* did *Chawcer.* And tho', perhaps, the love of their Masters, may have transported both too far, in the frequent use of them; yet in my Opinion, Obsolete Words may then be laudably reviv'd, when either they are more Sounding, or more Significant than those in practice: And when their Obscurity is taken away, by joining other Words to them which clear the Sense; according to the Rule of *Horace,* for the admission of new Words. But in both cases, a Moderation is to be observ'd, in the use of them: For unnecessary Coynage, as well as unnecessary Revival, runs into Affectation; a fault to be avoided on either hand. Neither will I Justifie *Milton* for his Blank Verse, tho' I may excuse him, by the example of *Hannibal Caro,* and other *Italians,* who have us'd it: For whatever Causes he alledges for the abolishing of Rhyme (which I have not now the leisure to examine) his own particular Reason is plainly this, that Rhyme was not his Talent; he had neither the Ease of doing it, nor the Graces of it; which is manifest in his *Juvenilia,* or Verses written in his Youth: Where his Rhyme is always constrain'd and forc'd, and comes hardly from him at an Age when the Soul is most pliant; and the Passion of Love, makes almost every Man a Rhymer, tho' not a Poet.

—John Dryden, "Discourse concerning the Original and Progress of Satire" (1693), *The Works of John Dryden,* ed. H. T. Swedenberg, Jr., et al. (Berkeley: University of California Press, 1974), Vol. 4, pp. 14–15

JOSEPH ADDISON ON THE HERO IN *PARADISE LOST*

[Joseph Addison (1672–1719) was a noted British poet and playwright but is today best known as a brilliant essayist whose articles are models of English prose. With Richard Steele (1672–1729), Addison issued such weekly periodical papers as *The Tatler* (1709–11) and *The Spectator* (1711–12). In this extract from one of a series of essays on Milton in *The Spectator,* Addison refutes John Dryden's claim (made in passing in his "Dedication" to *The Aeneis of Virgil,* 1697) that Milton had unwittingly made Satan the hero of *Paradise Lost.*]

There is another Objection against *Milton's* Fable, which is indeed almost the same with the former, tho' placed in a different Light, namely, That the Hero in the *Paradise Lost* is unsuccessful, and by no means a Match for his Enemies. This gave occasion to Mr. *Dryden's* Reflection, that the Devil was in reality *Milton's* Hero. I think I have obviated this Objection in my first Paper. The *Paradise Lost* is an Epic, or a Narrative Poem, and he that looks for an Hero in it, searches for that which *Milton* never intended; but if he will needs fix the Name of an

Hero upon any Person in it, 'tis certainly the *Messiah* who is the Hero, both in the Principal Action, and in the chief Episodes. Paganism could not furnish out a real Action for a Fable greater than that of the *Iliad* or *Æneid,* and therefore an Heathen could not form a higher Notion of a Poem than one of that kind, which they call an Heroic. Whether *Milton's* is not of a sublimer Nature I will not presume to determine: It is sufficient that I shew there is in the *Paradise Lost* all the Greatness of Plan, Regularity of Design, and masterly Beauties which we discover in *Homer* and *Virgil.*

I must in the next Place observe, that *Milton* has interwoven in the Texture of his Fable some Particulars which do not seem to have Probability enough for an Epic Poem, particularly in the Actions which he ascribes to *Sin* and *Death,* and the Picture which he draws of the *Lymbo of Vanity,* with other Passages in the second Book. Such Allegories rather savour of the Spirit of *Spencer* and *Ariosto,* than of *Homer* and *Virgil.*

In the Structure of his Poem he has likewise admitted of too many Digressions. It is finely observed by *Aristotle,* that the Author of an Heroic Poem should seldom speak himself, but throw as much of his Work as he can into the Mouths of those who are his Principal Actors. *Aristotle* has given no Reason for this Precept; but I presume it is because the Mind of the Reader is more awed and elevated when he hears *Æneas* or *Achilles* speak, then when *Virgil* or *Homer* talk in their own Persons. Besides that assuming the Character of an eminent Man is apt to fire the Imagination, and raise the Ideas of the Author. *Tully* tells us, mentioning his Dialogue of Old Age, in which *Cato* is the chief Speaker, that upon a Review of it he was agreeably imposed upon, and fancied that it was *Cato,* and not he himself, who utter'd his Thoughts on that Subject.

—Joseph Addison, *The Spectator* (9 February 1712), *The Spectator,* ed. Donald F. Bond (Oxford: Clarendon Press, 1965), Vol. 3, pp. 59–60

VOLTAIRE ON THE GREATNESS OF *PARADISE LOST*

[Voltaire was the pseudonym of François Marie Arouet (1694–1778), one of the leading figures in the French Enlightenment and the author of such celebrated works as the *Philosophical Dictionary* (1764) and *Candide* (1759). In this extract, taken from an essay written in English during his stay in England (1726–29), Voltaire remarks on the greatness of *Paradise Lost,* especially its loftiness of tone.]

'Paradise Lost' is the only poem wherein are to be found in a perfect degree that uniformity which satisfies the mind and that variety which pleases the imagination, all its episodes being necessary lines which aim at the center of a perfect circle. Where is the nation who would not be pleased with the interview of Adam and the Angel? With the mountain of vision, with the bold strokes which make up the relentless, undaunted and sly character of Satan? But above all with that sublime wisdom which Milton exerts, whenever he dares to describe God, and to make Him speak? He seems indeed to draw the picture of the Almighty, as like as human nature can reach to, through the mortal dust in which we are clouded.

The heathens always, the Jews often, and our Christian priests sometimes, represent God as a tyrant infinitely powerful. But the God of Milton is always a creator, a father, and a judge, nor is His vengeance jarring with His mercy, nor His predeterminations repugnant to the liberty of man. These are the pictures which lift up indeed the soul of the reader. Milton in that point as well as in many others is as far above the ancient poets as the Christian religion is above the heathen fables.

But he hath especially an indisputable claim to the unanimous admiration of mankind, when he descends from those high flights to the natural description of human things. It is observable that in all other poems love is represented as a vice; in Milton only it is a virtue. The pictures he draws of it are naked as the persons he speaks of, and as venerable. He removes with a chaste hand the veil which covers everywhere else the enjoyments of that passion. There is softness, tenderness and warmth without lasciviousness; the poet transports

himself and us into that state of innocent happiness in which
Adam and Eve continued for a short time: he soars not above
human, but above a corrupt nature, and as there is no instance
of such love, there is none of such poetry.

—François Marie Arouet (Voltaire), *The Epic Poetry of the
European Nations from Homer Down to Milton* (1727), rpt.
(abridged) as *Voltaire's Essay on Milton,* ed. Desmond Flower
(Cambridge: Printed Privately, 1954), pp. 4–5

SAMUEL JOHNSON ON MILTON'S IMAGINATION

[Samuel Johnson (1709–1784), perhaps the greatest
British literary figure of the eighteenth century, was a
poet, novelist, critic, and biographer of distinction.
Perhaps his most celebrated critical work is *Lives of the
English Poets* (1779–81), from which the following
extract is taken. Here, Johnson praises Milton's imagination as being uniformly lofty and sublime but criticizes *Paradise Lost* for depicting scenes beyond the
power of readers to envisage.]

He had considered creation in its whole extent, and his
descriptions are therefore learned. He had accustomed his
imagination to unrestrained indulgence, and his conceptions
therefore were extensive. The characteristick quality of his
poem is sublimity. He sometimes descends to the elegant, but
his element is the great. He can occasionally invest himself
with grace; but his natural port is gigantick loftiness. He can
please when pleasure is required; but it is his peculiar power
to astonish.

He seems to have been well acquainted with his own genius,
and to know what it was that Nature had bestowed upon him
more bountifully than upon others; the power of displaying the
vast, illuminating the splendid, enforcing the awful, darkening
the gloomy, and aggravating the dreadful: he therefore chose a

subject on which too much could not be said, on which he might tire his fancy without the censure of extravagance.

The appearances of nature, and the occurrences of life, did not satiate his appetite of greatness. To paint things as they are, requires a mute attention, and employs the memory rather than the fancy. Milton's delight was to sport in the wide regions of possibility; reality was a scene too narrow for his mind. He sent his faculties out upon discovery, into worlds where only the imagination can travel, and delighted to form new modes of existence, and furnish sentiment and action to superior beings, to trace the counsels of hell, or accompany the choirs of heaven.

But he could not be always in other worlds: he must sometimes revisit earth, and tell of things visible and known. When he cannot raise wonder by the sublimity of his mind, he gives delight by its fertility. ⟨. . .⟩

Pleasure and terror are indeed the genuine sources of poetry; but poetical pleasure must be such as human imagination can at least conceive, and poetical terrour such as human strength and fortitude may combat. The good and evil of Eternity are too ponderous for the wings of wit; the mind sinks under them in passive helplessness, content with calm belief and humble adoration.

Known truths, however, may take a different appearance, and be conveyed to the mind by a new train of intermediate images. This Milton has undertaken, and performed with pregnancy and vigour of mind peculiar to himself. Whoever considers the few radical positions which the Scriptures afforded him, will wonder by what energetick operation he expanded them to such extent, and ramified them to so much variety, restrained as he was by religious reverence from licentiousness of fiction.

Here is a full display of the united force of study and genius; of a great accumulation of materials, with judgement to digest, and fancy to combine them: Milton was able to select from nature, or from story, from ancient fable, or from modern science, whatever could illustrate or adorn his thoughts. An accumulation of knowledge impregnated his mind, fermented by study, and exalted by imagination.

It has been therefore said, without an indecent hyperbole, by one of his encomiasts, that in reading *Paradise Lost* we read a book of universal knowledge.

But original deficience cannot be supplied. The want of human interest is always felt. *Paradise Lost* is one of the books which the reader admires and lays down, and forgets to take up again. None ever wished it longer than it is. Its perusal is a duty rather than a pleasure. We read Milton for instruction, retire harassed and overburdened, and look elsewhere for recreation; we desert our master, and seek for companions.

> —Samuel Johnson, *Lives of the English Poets* (1779–81; rpt. London: Oxford University Press, 1906), Vol. 1, pp. 122–23, 126–27

THOMAS BABINGTON MACAULAY ON MILTON AND DANTE

[Thomas Babington Macaulay (1800–1859) was a distinguished essayist and reviewer before turning late in life to the writing of the *History of England* (1849–55). In this extract, Macaulay compares *Paradise Lost* with Dante's *The Divine Comedy,* attributing the differences between the two epics to differences in the temperaments of the two poets.]

The only poem of modern times which can be compared with the *Paradise Lost* is the *Divine Comedy*. The subject of Milton, in some points, resembled that of Dante; but he has treated it in a widely different manner. We cannot, we think, better illustrate our opinion respecting our own great poet, than by contrasting him with the father of Tuscan literature. ⟨. . .⟩

The character of Milton was peculiarly distinguished by loftiness of spirit; that of Dante by intensity of feeling. In every line of the *Divine Comedy* we discern the asperity which is produced by pride struggling with misery. There is perhaps no work in the world so deeply and so uniformly sorrowful. The melancholy of Dante was no fantastic caprice. It was not, as far as at this distance of time can be judged, the effect of external circumstances. It was from within. Neither love nor glory, neither the conflicts of earth nor the hope of heaven could dispel it. It turned every consolation and every pleasure into its own nature. It resembled that noxious Sardinian soil of which the intense bitterness is said to have been perceptible even in its honey. His mind was, in the noble language of the Hebrew poet, "a land of darkness, as darkness itself, and where the light was as darkness." The gloom of his character discolours all the passions of men, and all the face of nature, and tinges with its own livid hue the flowers of Paradise and the glories of the eternal throne. All the portraits of him are singularly characteristic. No person can look on the features, noble even to ruggedness, the dark furrows of the cheek, the haggard and woful stare of the eye, the sullen and contemptuous curve of the lip, and doubt that they belong to a man too proud and too sensitive to be happy.

Milton was, like Dante, a statesman and a lover; and, like Dante, he had been unfortunate in ambition and in love. He had survived his health and his sight, the comforts of his home, and the prosperity of his party. Of the great men by whom he had been distinguished at his entrance into life, some had been taken away from the evil to come; some had carried into foreign climates their unconquerable hatred of oppression; some were pining in dungeons; and some had poured forth their blood on scaffolds. Venal and licentious scribblers, with just sufficient talent to clothe the thoughts of a pandar in the style of a bellman, were now the favourite writers of the Sovereign and of the public. It was a loathsome herd, which could be compared to nothing so fitly as to the rabble of *Comus*, grotesque monsters, half bestial half human, dropping with wine, bloated with gluttony, and reeling in obscene dances. Amidst these that fair Muse was placed, like the chaste lady of the Masque, lofty, spotless, and serene, to be chattered at, and pointed at, and grinned at, by the whole rout of Satyrs and Goblins. If ever despondency and asperity could be excused in any man, they might have been excused in Milton. But the strength of his mind overcame everyday calamity. Neither blindness, nor gout, nor age, nor penury, nor domestic afflictions, nor political disappointments, nor abuse, nor proscription, nor neglect, had power to disturb his sedate and majestic patience. His spirits do not seem to have been high, but they were similarly equable. His temper was serious, perhaps stern; but it was a temper which no sufferings could render sullen or fretful. Such as it was when, on the eve of great events, he returned from his travels, in the prime of health and manly beauty, loaded with literary distinctions, and glowing with patriotic hopes, such it continued to be when, after having experienced every calamity which is incident to our nature, old, poor, sightless and disgraced, he retired to his hovel to die.

Hence it was that, though he wrote the *Paradise Lost* at a time of life when images of beauty and tenderness are in general beginning to fade, even from those minds in which they have not been effaced by anxiety and disappointment, he adorned it with all that is most lovely and delightful in the physical and in the moral world. Neither Theocritus nor Ariosto had a finer or a more healthful sense of the pleasantness of external objects, or loved better to luxuriate amidst sunbeams and flowers, the songs of nightingales, the juice of summer fruits, and the coolness of shady fountains. His conception of love unites all the voluptuousness of the Oriental harem, and all the gallantry of the chivalric tournament, with all the pure and quiet affection of an English fireside. His poetry reminds us of the miracles of Alpine scenery. Nooks and dells, beautiful as fairy land, are embossed in its most rugged and gigantic elevations. The roses and myrtles bloom unchilled on the verge of the avalanche.

—Thomas Babington Macaulay, "Milton" (1825), *Critical, Historical, and Miscellaneous Essays* (Boston: Houghton Mifflin, 1860), Vol. 1, pp. 220, 230–32

STOPFORD A. BROOKE ON THE COSMOGRAPHY OF *PARADISE LOST*

[Stopford A. Brooke (1832–1916) was a prolific British literary critic. Among his books are *English Literature* (1898) and *Naturalism in English Poetry* (1920). In this extract from his study of Milton, Brooke describes the relationship between Heaven, Hell, and our world.]

The Universe in *Paradise Lost* consists of Heaven or the Empyrean, of Hell, of Chaos, and of our World.

Heaven is on high, indefinitely extended, and walled towards Chaos with a crystal wall, having opal towers and sapphire battlements. In the wall a vast gate opens on Chaos, and from it runs a broad and ample road, "powdered with stars," whose dust is gold, to the throne of God. The throne is in the midst of Heaven, high on the sacred hill, lost in ineffable light. In the hill is a cave whence the alternate light and shade of heaven proceed, for the angels rest in sleep and wake to work. Around the hill is the vast plain clothed with flowers, watered by living streams among the trees of life, where on great days the angelic assembly meets; and nearer to the hill is the pavement like a sea of jasper. Beyond, are vast regions, where are the blissful bowers of "amarantine shade, fountain, or spring;" among which in the fellowships of joy sit the sons of light. The trees bear ambrosial fruitage and the vines nectar; the ground is covered each morn with pearly rain and the boughs with mellifluous dews. In the midst is the Fount of Life, shaded by the leaves and flowers of the Tree of Life, that also grows

> where the river of Bliss through midst of Heav'n
> Rolls o'er Elysian flow'rs her amber stream.

These regions extend infinitely, as varied in landscape as the earth—tree-clad hills and vales, woods, streams and plains; and among them the archangels have their royal seats built as Satan's was, far-blazing on a hill, of diamond quarries and of golden rocks.

Chaos is opened on by the great gate. It is a vastly immeasurable abyss—

> Outrageous as a sea, dark, wasteful, wild,
> Up from the bottom turned by furious winds
> And surging waves.

Hot, cold, moist, and dry strive here for mastery. It is "the womb of Nature, and perhaps her grave."—Noises loud and ruinous fill it, but the loudest noise is where, on its frontiers, towards Heaven, Chaos and his consort Night, amid the warring elements, keep their pavilion.

Hell lies in the depths of Chaos, a fall of nine days and nights from Heaven. In its midst, and it is conceived as circular, is the bottomless lake of fire, into which pour the four rivers, Acheron, Phlegeton, Styx, and Cocytus. Around the lake a vast space of dry land extends, formed of solid fire, in one of whose hills Pandemonium was formed entire, and rose out of it, when formed, like an exhalation. The City of Hell is afterwards built round Pandemonium on this dry ground of fire, and the country round the city is broken with rock, and valley, and hill, and plain. Further on, in another concentric band, we catch a glimpse of a desert land, seemingly moist, but giving no relief; full of rocks, caves, lakes, fens, bogs, dens, and shades of death, round which Lethe, like the fabled Ocean stream, flows in a circle, and environs Hell. After that is the realm of cold,

> Beyond this flood, a frozen continent
> Lies dark and wild, beat with perpetual storms
> Of whirlwind and dire hail—

a land of snow and ice, deep as the Serbonian bog, over which Satan soars high on his way to the gate, and the cold of which is as fire. Then come the bounds of Hell, and the three-folded gates. Over all is the concave vault of fire. This is Milton's geography of Hell, within four concentric circles.

Our World as Milton calls it, the whole solar system and the stars, is linked to Heaven and to Hell, and in Chaos. It is a vast hollow sphere, hung at its zenith by a golden chain from the Empyrean. Its lowest point is distant from Hell as far as one of the radii extend. It is this dark globe that Satan sees from Chaos, by the light of Heaven, and on its outer round he alights, as on a continent of waste land. It is beaten by the winds of Chaos and has only light on that side of it which is turned to Heaven. At its very zenith a bright sea flows as of liquid pearl, from which a mighty structure of stairs leads up to Heaven's gate. Over against the stairs a passage down to the Earth opens into the hollow sphere. At this opening Satan looks in upon the starry heavens of all this world, which fill the "calm firmament," and flies amongst innumerable stars to the Sun and thence to Earth the central point of the nine spheres.

Milton accepts then for his poetic uses the Ptolemaic system, of which the earth was the centre. Around the Earth revolved the spheres of the Seven planets, the Moon, Mercury, Venus, the Sun, Mars, Jupiter, and Saturn. The eighth sphere was the firmament of the Fixed Stars, the ninth or Crystalline Sphere, was inclosed in the tenth the Primum Mobile or the First Moved, the last of the hollow shell. They all circled round the Earth with "a complex combination of their separate motions invented to explain the phenomena of the heavens." This is Milton's "*World.*" When the souls who are destined to the Paradise of Fools fly upwards, Bk. iii. 481,

> They pass the planets seven, and pass the fixed,
> And that crystalline sphere whose balance weighs
> The trepidation talked, and that first moved.

He uses this scheme because it suited his poetic imagination, and because it was the scheme accepted by his youth. But he had seen Galileo in 1638, and says he "was a prisoner to the Inquisition for thinking in astronomy otherwise than the Franciscan and Dominican licensers thought," and more than twenty years afterwards, during which one may suppose he did not neglect to gain knowledge, he makes Raphael sketch for Adam the Copernican system (viii. 15–178) and shows his own knowledge in it (iv. 593–97). The angel hints that the question is obscure, but it is plain that whatever Milton professed, Raphael followed Copernicus. The Ptolemaic system is not adopted then by Milton because he held it to be the clearly right view of the universe, but because it was suited to his poetical wants. Lastly, as this vast sphere was linked to Heaven by its chain and staircase, so it was linked to Hell by the mighty causeway which Sin and Death had beaten together out of

Chaos; high arched, and made fast with pins of adamant and chains to the outside base of this round world.
—Stopford A. Brooke, *Milton* (New York: D. Appleton, 1885), pp. 84–87

WALTER RALEIGH ON MILTON'S THEOLOGICAL BELIEFS

[Walter Raleigh (1861–1922) was the first holder of the chair of English literature at Oxford University. He is the author of *The English Novel* (1894), *Style* (1897), *Shakespeare* (1907), and other works. In this extract from *Milton* (1900), Raleigh notes that many of Milton's theological views expressed in *Paradise Lost* are not orthodox but may have been partially inspired by the imaginative requirements of his poem.]

It seems likely that Milton himself, before he was fairly caught in the mesh of his own imagination, was well aware that his subject demanded something of the nature of a *tour-de-force*. He had to give physical, geometric embodiment to a far-reaching scheme of abstract speculation and thought,—parts of it very reluctant to such a treatment. The necessities of the epic form constrained him. When Satan, on the top of Mount Niphates, exclaims—

Which way I fly is Hell; myself am Hell;

when Michael promises to Adam, after his expulsion from the garden—

A Paradise within thee; happier far;

Milton must have known as well as any of his critics that this conception of Hell and Paradise, if insisted on, would have shattered the fabric of his poem. His figures of Sin and Death were of his own invention, and we must not suppose him so obtuse as never to have realized the part that his shaping

imagination bore in the presentment of other and greater figures in the poem. In some respects he tried rather to impose a
scheme of thought and imagination upon his age than to
express the ideas that he found current. His theology and his
cosmical conceptions are equally tainted with his individual
heresies. He flies in the face of the Athanasian Creed by representing the generation of the Son as an event occurring in time
—"on such a day as Heaven's great year brings forth." His later
poem of *Paradise Regained* and the posthumous treatise of
Christian Doctrine show him an Arian; in the poem the
Almighty is made to speak of

> This perfect man, by merit called my Son.

His account of the creation of the World as a mere ordering or
re-arrangement of the wild welter of an uncreated material
Chaos receives no countenance from the Fathers. In many
points of theological teaching he is compelled to form definite
and even visual conceptions where orthodoxy had cautiously
confined itself to vague general propositions. So that the
description of Sin and Death and of the causeway built by them
between Hell-gates and the World, much as it has been object-
ed to even by admirers of the poem, is only an extreme
instance of the defining and hardening process that Milton
found needful throughout for the concrete presentment of the
high doings which are his theme. He congealed the mysteries
of Time and Space, Love and Death, Sin and Forgiveness, into a
material system; and in so doing, while paying the utmost def-
erence to his authorities, he yet exercised many a choice with
regard to matters indifferent or undefinable. Thus, for instance,
he borrows from the Talmud the notion that Satan first learned
the existence of a prohibited tree from overhearing a conversation between Adam and Eve. He was surely conscious of what
he was doing, and would have been not ill-pleased to learn
that the Universe, as he conceived of it, has since been called
by his name. It is Milton's Paradise Lost, lost by Milton's Adam
and Eve, who are tempted by Milton's Satan, and punished by
Milton's God. The stamp of his clear, hard imagination is on the
whole fabric; and it is not much harder for us to coax ourselves
into the belief that his is indeed the very world we inhabit than
it was for the men of his own time. The senses and the intellect

are older than modern science, and were employed to good effect before the invention of the spectroscope; it is they in their daily operation that make it difficult to leap the gulf which separates the amenities and trivialities of common life from the solemn theatre of the poet's imagination. The objection that the poem has lost much of its value because we are compelled to imagine where our elders believed is of little weight in a case like this, where our lack of belief is not brought home to us until insuperable difficulties are placed in the way of our imagination. Where Milton was freest, there we follow him most gladly; where he wrote in fetters, as notably in some of the scenes transacted in Heaven, our imagination, not our belief, is the first to rebel.

> —Walter Raleigh, *Milton* (London: Edward Arnold, 1900), pp. 81–84

T. S. Eliot on Milton's Rhetoric

[T. S. Eliot (1888–1965), the American poet who spent the majority of his adult life in England, is best known as the leading figure of the Modernist movement in the 1920s and the author of *The Waste Land* (1922). Eliot was, however, also a prolific and penetrating critic. In this extract, Eliot studies Milton's poetic style, noting its emphasis on sound and rhetoric.]

⟨. . .⟩ it is not so unfair, as it might at first appear, to say that Milton writes English like a dead language. The criticism has been made with regard to his involved syntax. But a tortuous style, when its peculiarity is aimed at precision (as with Henry James), is not necessarily a dead one; only when the complication is dictated by a demand of verbal music, instead of by any demand of sense.

> Thrones, dominations, princedoms, virtues, powers,
> If these magnific titles yet remain
> Not merely titular, since by decree
> Another now hath to himself engrossed

All power, and us eclipsed under the name
Of King anointed, for whom all this haste
Of midnight march, and hurried meeting here,
This only to consult how we may best
With what may be devised of honours new
Receive him coming to receive from us
Knee-tribute yet unpaid, prostration vile,
Too much to one, but double how endured,
To one and to his image now proclaimed?

With which compare:

'However, he didn't mind thinking that if Cissy should prove all that was likely enough their having a subject in common couldn't but practically conduce; though the moral of it all amounted rather to a portent, the one that Haughty, by the same token, had done least to reassure him against, of the extent to which the native jungle harboured the female specimen and to which its ostensible cover, the vast level of mixed growths stirred wavingly in whatever breeze, was apt to be identifiable but as an agitation of the latest redundant thing in ladies' hats.'

This quotation, taken almost at random from *The Ivory Tower,* is not intended to represent Henry James at any hypothetical 'best', any more than the noble passage from *Paradise Lost* is meant to be Milton's hypothetical worst. The question is the difference of intention, in the elaboration of styles both of which depart so far from lucid simplicity. The sound, of course, is never irrelevant, and the style of James certainly depends for its effect a good deal on the sound of a voice, James's own, painfully explaining. But the complication, with James, is due to a determination not to simplify, and in that simplification lose any of the real intricacies and by-paths of mental movement; whereas the complication of Miltonic sentence is an active complication, a complication deliberately introduced into what was a previously simplified and abstract thought. The dark angel here is not *thinking* or conversing, but making a speech carefully prepared for him; and the arrangement is for the sake of musical value, not for significance. A straightforward utterance, as of a Homeric or Dantesque character, would make the speaker very much more real to us; but reality is no part of the intention. We have in fact to read such a passage not analytically, to get the poetic impression. I am not suggesting that Milton has no idea to convey which he regards as important: only that the syntax is determined by the musical significance, by the auditory imagination, rather than by the attempt to follow actual speech or thought. It is at least more nearly possible to distinguish the pleasure which arises from the *noise,* from the pleasure due to other elements, than with the verse of Shakespeare, in which the auditory imagination and the imagination of the other senses are more nearly fused, and fused together with the thought. The result with Milton is, in one sense of the word, *rhetoric.* That term is not intended to be derogatory. This kind of 'rhetoric' is not necessarily bad in its influence; but it may be considered bad in relation to the historical life of a language as a whole. I have said elsewhere that the living English which was Shakespeare's became split up into two components one of which was exploited by Milton and the other by Dryden. Of the two, I still think Dryden's development the healthier, because it was Dryden who preserved, so far as it was preserved at all, the tradition of conversational language in poetry: and I might add that it seems to me easier to get back to healthy language from Dryden than it is to get back to it from Milton. For what such a generalization is worth, Milton's influence on the eighteenth century was much more deplorable than Dryden's.

—T. S. Eliot, *Milton: Two Studies* (London: Faber & Faber, 1936), pp. 14–17

C. S. Lewis on the Nature of Satan

[C. S. Lewis (1898–1963), a longtime fellow of Magdalen College, Oxford, was a prolific essayist, critic, novelist, and Christian apologist. Among his critical works are *The Allegory of Love* (1936) and *English Literature in the Sixteenth Century* (1954). In this extract from *A Preface to* Paradise Lost (1942), Lewis ponders the nature of Satan and why he is such a compelling figure in *Paradise Lost.*]

What we see in Satan is the horrible co-existence of a subtle and incessant intellectual activity with an incapacity to understand anything. This doom he has brought upon himself; in order to avoid seeing one thing he has, almost voluntarily, incapacitated himself from seeing at all. And thus, throughout the poem, all his torments come, in a sense, at his own bidding, and the Divine judgement might have been expressed in the words '*thy* will be done'. He says 'Evil be thou my good' (which includes 'Nonsense be thou my sense') and his prayer is granted. It is by his own will that he revolts; but not by his own will that Revolt itself tears its way in agony out of his head and becomes a being separable from himself, capable of enchanting him (II, 749–66) and bearing him unexpected and unwelcome progeny. By his own will he becomes a serpent in Book IX; in Book X he is a serpent whether he will or no. This progressive degradation, of which he himself is vividly aware, is carefully marked in the poem. He begins by fighting for 'liberty', however misconceived; but almost at once sinks to fighting for 'Honour, Dominion, glorie, and renoune' (VI, 422). Defeated in this, he sinks to that great design which makes the main subject of the poem—the design of ruining two creatures who had never done him any harm, no longer in the serious hope of victory, but only to annoy the Enemy whom he cannot directly attack. (The coward in Beaumont and Fletcher's play, not daring to fight a duel, decided to go home and beat his servants.) This brings him as a spy into the universe, and soon not even a political spy, but a mere peeping Tom leering and writhing in prurience as he overlooks the privacy of two lovers, and there described, almost for the first time in the poem, not as the fallen Archangel or Hell's dread Emperor, but simply as 'the Devil' (IV, 502)—the salacious grotesque, half bogey and half buffoon, of popular tradition. From hero to general, from general to politician, from politician to secret service agent, and thence to a thing that peers in at bedroom or bathroom windows, and thence to a toad, and finally to a snake—such is the progress of Satan. This progress, misunderstood, has given rise to the belief that Milton began by making Satan more glorious than he intended and then, too late, attempted to rectify the error. But such an unerring picture of the 'sense of injured merit' in its actual operations upon character cannot have come about by blundering and accident. We need not doubt that it was the poet's intention to be fair to evil, to give it a run for its money—to show it *first* at the height, with all its rants and melodrama and 'Godlike imitated state' about it, and *then* to trace what actually becomes of such self-intoxication when it encounters reality. Fortunately we happen to know that the terrible soliloquy in Book IV (32–113) was conceived and in part composed before the first two books. It was from this conception that Milton started and when he put the most specious aspects of Satan at the very beginning of his poem he was relying on two predispositions in the minds of his readers, which in that age, would have guarded them from our later misunderstanding. Men still believed that there really was such a person as Satan, and that he was a liar. The poet did not foresee that his work would one day meet the disarming simplicity of critics who take for gospel things said by the father of falsehood in public speeches to his troops.

It remains, of course, true that Satan is the best drawn of Milton's characters. The reason is not hard to find. Of the major characters whom Milton attempted he is incomparably the easiest to draw. Set a hundred poets to tell the same story and in ninety of the resulting poems Satan will be the best character. In all but a few writers the 'good' characters are the least successful, and every one who has ever tried to make even the humblest story ought to know why. To make a character worse than oneself it is only necessary to release imaginatively from control some of the bad passions which, in real life, are always straining at the leash; the Satan, the Iago, the Becky Sharp, within each of us, is always there and only too ready, the moment the leash is slipped, to come out and have in our books that holiday we try to deny them in our lives. But if you try to draw a character better than yourself, all you can do is to take the best moments you have had and to imagine them prolonged and more consistently embodied in action. But the real high virtues which we do not possess at all we cannot depict except in a purely external fashion. We do not really know what it feels like to be a man much better than ourselves. His whole inner landscape is one we have never seen, and when we guess it we blunder. It is in their 'good' characters that novelists make, unawares, the most shocking self-revelations. Heaven understands Hell and Hell does not understand

Heaven, and all of us, in our measure, share the Satanic, or at least the Napoleonic, blindness. To project ourselves into a wicked character, we have only to stop doing something, and something that we are already tired of doing; to project ourselves into a good one we have to do what we cannot and become what we are not. Hence all that is said about Milton's 'sympathy' with Satan, his expression in Satan of his own pride, malice, folly, misery, and lust, is true in a sense, but not in a sense peculiar to Milton. The Satan in Milton enables him to draw the character well just as the Satan in us enables us to receive it. Not as Milton, but as man, he has trodden the burning marl, pursued vain war with heaven, and turned aside with leer malign. A fallen man *is* very like a fallen angel. That, indeed, is one of the things which prevents the Satanic predicament from becoming comic. It is too near us; and doubtless Milton expected all readers to perceive that in the long run either the Satanic predicament or else the delighted obedience of Messiah, of Abdiel, of Adam, and of Eve, must be their own. It is therefore right to say that Milton has put much of himself into Satan; but it is unwarrantable to conclude that he was pleased with that part of himself or expected us to be pleased. Because he was, like the rest of us, damnable, it does not follow that he was, like Satan, damned.

—C. S. Lewis, *A Preface to* Paradise Lost (London: Oxford University Press, 1942), pp. 99–101

DAVID DAICHES ON MILTON AND CHRISTIAN HUMANISM

[David Daiches (b. 1912), University Lecturer in English and fellow of Jesus College, Cambridge, is a distinguished Scottish literary critic and the author of *Robert Burns* (1950), *A Critical History of English Literature* (1960), and other works. In this extract from *Milton* (1957), Daiches maintains that *Paradise Lost* is a product of Milton's Christian humanism and also a synthesis of biblical, classical, mediaeval, and modern literary modes.]

Paradise Lost shows Milton as Christian humanist using all the resources of the European literary tradition that had come down to him—biblical, classical, mediaeval, renaissance; pagan, Jewish and Christian. Imagery from classical fable and mediaeval romance, allusion to myths, legends and stories of all kinds, geographical imagery deriving from Milton's own fascination with books of travel and echoes of the Elizabethan excitement at the new discoveries, biblical history and doctrine, rabbinical and patristic learning—all these and more are found in this great synthesis of all that the Western mind was stored with by the middle of the seventeenth century. Like *The Faerie Queene,* Milton's epic is a great synthesizing poem, but Milton's synthesis is more successful than Spenser's because he places his different kinds of knowledge—biblical, classical, mediaeval, modern—in a logical hierarchy, and never mingles, as Spenser often does, classical myth and biblical story on equal terms. If all the resources of classical mythology are employed in order to build up an overwhelming picture of the beauty of Eden before the Fall, that is because Milton is saying that here, and here only, were all the yearnings of men for ideal gardens fully realized. The description of Eden in Book IV is indeed one of the finest examples of Milton's use of pagan classical imagery for a clearly defined Christian purpose:

> The Birds thir quire apply; airs, vernal airs,
> Breathing the smell of field and grove, attune
> The trembling leaves, while Universal *Pan*
> Knit with the *Graces* and the *Hours* in dance
> Led on th' Eternal Spring. Not that fair field
> Of *Enna,* where *Proserpin* gathring flowrs
> Her self a fairer Flowre by gloomie *Dis*
> Was gathered, which cost *Ceres* all that pain
> To seek her through the world; nor that sweet Grove
> Of *Daphne* by *Orontes,* and th' inspir'd
> *Castalian* Spring, might with this Paradise
> Of *Eden* strive; . . .

There is a tremulous glory in this description of ideal Nature fully realized, and repetitions such as 'airs, vernal airs', and 'Proserpin gathring flowrs / Her self a fairer Flowre' help to give the proper emotional quality to the verse. The classical imagery is neither purely decorative nor as solidly grounded in reality as the biblical groundwork of the story: Milton uses myth for what it is, the imaginative projection of all man's deepest hopes and fears. Matthew Arnold cited the lines about Proserpine and Ceres as a touchstone of great poetry, but did not pause to inquire why. It is in the combined suggestion of infinite beauty and of foreboding and loss that Milton manages to capture the plangent sense of transience which accompanies all postlapsarian response to beauty, and thus even while describing a prelapsarian scene he introduces overtones of the Fall. And more than that—these overtones emphasize a paradox that lies at the very heart of *Paradise Lost,* namely that only after one has lost something ideally lovely can its true worth be known, so that the Fall is necessary that we may pursue the ideal, in the teeth of all the obstacles that now confront us, with a deeper sense of its desirability.

> —David Daiches, *Milton* (London: Hutchinson University Library, 1957), pp. 151–53

WILLIAM EMPSON ON MILTON AND GOD

[William Empson (1906–1984) was a leading British literary critic and theorist. His works include *Seven Types of Ambiguity* (1930), *Some Versions of Pastoral* (1935), and *Milton's God* (1961), from which the following extract is taken. Here, Empson argues that Milton's statement, at the beginning of *Paradise Lost,* that he wishes to "justify the ways of God to men" suggests Milton's belief that God is a morally ambiguous figure.]

Milton genuinely considered God in need of defence, and indeed that, when Milton said at the beginning of his epic he intended to justify God, he was so far from expecting a reader to think the phrase poetical rhetoric that he was not even stepping out of the usual procedure of his prose. A curious trick has been played on modern readers here; they are told: 'Why, but of course you must read the poem taking for granted that

Milton's God is good; not to do that would be absurdly unhistorical. Why, the first business of a literary critic is to sink his mind wholly into the mental world of the author, and in a case like this you must accept what they all thought way back in early times.' I think this literary doctrine is all nonsense anyhow; a critic ought to use his own moral judgement, for what it is worth, as well as try to understand the author's, and that is the only way he can arrive at 'total reaction'. But in a case like this the argument is also grossly unhistorical. No doubt Milton would only have snorted if a Victorian had come up and praised him for making Satan good, but anyone who told him he had made God wicked would find his mind surprisingly at home; there would be some severe cross-questioning (is this a Jesuit or merely an Arminian?), but if that passed off all right he would ask the visitor to sit down and discuss the point at length. Nor was it only the later Milton, after the disillusion of the Fall of the Commonwealth, who felt God to need defence; he can be shown feeling it both before and after a major change in this theology. In *The Doctrine and Discipline of Divorce* (1643), writing as a believer in predestination, he remarks of Jesuits and Arminians that, if they could only understand the argument he has just propounded, 'they might, methinks, be persuaded to absolve both God and us' (*us* meaning the Calvinists). Near the end of Chapter III of the *De Doctrina* we find he has abandoned predestination, and his reason for it is still that he is anxious to absolve God:

> free causes are not impeded by law of necessity arising from the decrees or prescience of God. There are some who, in their zeal to oppose this doctrine, do not hesitate even to assert that God himself is the cause and origin of evil. Such men, if they are not to be looked upon as misguided rather than mischievous, should be ranked among the most abandoned of the blasphemers. An attempt to refute them would be nothing more than an argument to prove that God was not the evil spirit.

This exasperation against his opponents, this extreme readiness to see that they are making God into the Devil, while the point of distinction he wants to insist upon is really so very slight, makes evident that Milton himself was sensitive and anxious about the danger of finding that he too was worshipping the Devil. When Milton gets round to his own pronouncement on this point, in Chapter VIII, after listing the crucial texts, he is hardly able to do more than issue a rule of decorum:

> But though in these, as well as in many other passages of the Old and New Testaments, God distinctly declares that it is himself who impels the sinner to sin, who binds his understanding, and leads him into error; yet, on account of the infinite holiness of the Deity, it is not allowable to consider him as in the smallest instance the author of sin.

What first struck me, when I began to nose about in the English translation of the *De Doctrina*, rather belatedly, was that its tone is very unlike what the learned critics who summarize it had led me to expect. But maybe, I thought, having no judgement of Latin style, this is only a result of translation; the work was done by Sumner, later an Anglican bishop, who must have been working fairly rapidly; it was printed (and reviewed by Macaulay) in 1825, two years after the Latin text had been discovered. One can imagine a translator making it sound like Gibbon, partly because that was an easy formula but also through feeling a certain impatience with this heretic. But the following passage, from Chapter VII, 'Of the Creation', another discussion of the effects of the Fall, seemed to me enough to refute the suspicion; it rises above the variations of tone available to a translator:

> But, it is contended, God does not create souls impure, but only impaired in their nature, and destitute of original righteousness; I answer that to create pure souls, destitute of original righteousness,—to send them into contaminated and corrupt bodies,—to deliver them up in their innocence and helplessness to the prison house of the body, as to an enemy, with understanding blinded and with will enslaved,—in other words, wholly deprived of sufficient strength for resisting the vicious propensities of the body—to create souls thus circumstanced, would argue as much injustice, as to have created them impure would have argued impurity; it would have argued as much injustice, as to have created the first man Adam himself impaired in his nature, and destitute of original righteousness.

Surely, in the face of this burning sense of the injustice of God, which Milton only just manages to drag into line, it was rather absurd of C. S. Lewis to say that nobody had ever doubted Milton's account of the Fall until the Romantics made rebellion fashionable. A sympathetic reader of Milton's prose is accus-

tomed to feel that he writes like a lawyer or a politician, concerned to convince his reader by any argument which would
serve, though really more humane or enlightened arguments
are what have made Milton himself choose the side he is arguing on. But in discussing the justice of God Milton admits that
the conscience of every decent man is against what he has to
maintain; there is an 'outcry' against it; but what he has found
in the Bible is the horrible truth about the justice of God, and
men had much better learn to face it.

—William Empson, *Milton's God* (London: Chatto & Windus,
1961), pp. 204–7

CHRISTOPHER RICKS ON MILTON'S STYLE

[Christopher Ricks (b. 1933) is a British literary critic
who is now professor of English at Boston University.
He has written *English Drama to 1710* (1971), *T. S.
Eliot and Prejudice* (1988), and *Tennyson* (1989). In this
extract from *Milton's Grand Style* (1963), Ricks finds
that Milton's "grand style" is a fusion of grandeur and
subtlety.]

There is always the danger in discussing Milton's Grand Style of
assuming that it is merely grand, of conceding too much, of
leaning over backwards not to make claims. Professor Kenneth
Muir, for instance, is unnecessarily magnanimous on Milton's
behalf when he says that 'it is futile to expect the nervous energy, the subtle involutions of style, the tentacular imagery, the
linguistic daring and the colloquial ease of Shakespeare's best
verse'. This is true, if it means no more than that Shakespeare's
best verse is better than anyone else's. But beyond that—no,
Milton's style *does* command nervous energy, subtle involutions, tentacular imagery, and linguistic daring—though these
often take unShakespearian forms. (Colloquial ease we may
dispense with, as an extraordinary critical shibboleth.)

Yet Milton's grandeur and his subtlety (my concern in the
next chapter) often co-exist in the very same lines, which

makes it particularly important not to cordon off the poem from meddling practical critics. The following lines would generally be agreed to belong to Milton's sterner style, but their bareness is combined with local subtlety to produce an effect of astonishing breadth and power:

> So glister'd the dire Snake, and into fraud
> Led Eve our credulous Mother, to the Tree
> Of prohibition, root of all our woe.   (IX. 643–5)

These lines stamp themselves at once as in the Grand Style. What is remarkable, though, is that they are verbally subtle and active without any fussiness or any blurring of the grand austerity. I am thinking not only of the sombre gleam in the pun on *root*; but also of subtler effects: the playing of the bright *glister'd* against the dark *dire*, for instance. Or the superb use of the curt 'snake'. (Milton calls it the serpent fifteen times in Book IX; but the snake only three times: once literally, before Satan enters it; and twice with calculated brutality: 'So talk'd the spirited sly Snake', and here.)

There is the superbly suggestive diction: 'our credulous Mother', which must be one of the finest, most delicate, and most moving of all the oxymorons in the poem. A mother ought to be everything that is reliable and wise—here she is credulous. And *our* clinches the effect; *credulous* is pinioned on each side ('our . . . Mother'), and the full tragic pathos of the oxymoron is released. Sylvester's Du Bartas has two unusually good lines using 'credulous', but in the end how much smaller they are:

> poor Woman, wavering, weak, unwise,
> Light, credulous, news-lover, giv'n to lies.

There is the majesty of 'the Tree of prohibition'—no mere stilted Latinism, since it is literally true: the Tree is not just 'the prohibited Tree', but the Tree of *all* prohibition. And there is at this fatal moment the ringing echo of the opening lines of the poem in 'all our woe'. But perhaps the most irresistible of all the effects here is syntactical. 'Into fraud led Eve . . .' overlaps magnificently with '. . . led Eve to the Tree', so that what begins as a moving and ancient moral metaphor (lead us not into temptation) crystallizes with terrifying literalness. There is a touching change of focus, superbly compressed and yet without a shock or a jerk.

But the astonishing thing is not that these excellent explicable subtleties are there, but that they do not at all disturb the lines' serene, almost Dantesque, austerity. Milton, as so often, combines what are apparently incompatible greatnesses. Hazlitt remarked that 'the fervour of his imagination melts down and renders malleable, as in a furnace, the most contradictory materials'.

Clearly even those passages which are most in the Grand Style may also contain riches of a different kind. Macaulay was right to insist on how many and varied are the excellences of Milton's style, 'that style, which no rival has been able to equal, and no parodist to degrade, which displays in their highest perfection the idiomatic powers of the English tongue, and to which every ancient and every modern language has contributed something of grace, of energy, or of music'.
    —Christopher Ricks, *Milton's Grand Style* (Oxford: Clarendon Press, 1963), pp. 75–77

ANNE DAVIDSON FERRY ON MILTON'S NARRATOR IN *PARADISE LOST*

[Anne Davidson Ferry (b. 1930) is a professor of English at Boston College and the author of The *"Inward"* Language: Sonnets of Wyatt, Sidney, Shakespeare, Donne (1983) and The Art of Naming (1988). In this extract from her study of Paradise Lost (1967), Ferry comments on the narrator of this epic poem.]

When Milton recreated *Adam unparadiz'd* into *Paradise Lost* he could not simply transpose dramatic scenes into narrative form. He had to invent a narrator capable of telling his story in a manner expressive of its meaning. The commonly accepted tradition that Moses was the inspired author of Genesis would have made him the most obvious choice for such a narrator, and indeed in his earliest outline for a drama about the Fall of man, Milton intended to have the "invisible" world of innocence presented to his fallen audiences by Moses. Yet in the epic Milton chose to ignore that tradition, to reject that narrator, inventing instead a special voice designed to express his special interpretation of the story of Adam's Fall. That narrative voice, as bard and especially as blind bard, is perhaps Milton's most brilliant creation. It gives to *Paradise Lost* its remarkable completeness. Everything in the poem is contained within the circle of the narrator's vision, and it is the scope, the inclusiveness, and the complexity of that vision which gives the epic its scope, the inclusiveness, and the complexity of that vision which gives the epic its scope, inclusiveness, and complexity. It is also the nature of the narrative and his characteristic tone of voice which creates the impression we have when we read *Paradise Lost* of the poem's absolute uniqueness. There is no other speaker in English literature who stands in the same relation to his characters and his readers, no voice which uses quite the tone sustained throughout Milton's epic.

Just as the omnipresence of the narrator prevents us from reading *Paradise Lost* as a play, the nature of the speaker and his role prevent us from reading the epic as we are accustomed to read a novel. The relation among narrator, characters, and reader in the English novel is traditionally social. The style in which we are addressed as readers of fiction echoes, at the same time that it may also criticize, our daily speech; the language of narration bears some relation to realistic idiom. The tone of the speaker in the novel is measured by our social modes of private conversation or of public discourse.

Milton in *Paradise Lost* avoids either of these large possibilities because the relation of the speaker to his characters and his readers is not social, and therefore his language could not be either the language of private conversation or of public speech. The speaker is "from the chearful waies of men / Cut off" by his blindness. He is specifically excluded from our society by his special suffering and his special gift, which enable him to penetrate the surface of our fragmentary lives to a vision of essential, eternal relationships, of the circular order of God's universe. His language must therefore strip itself of purely local detail, of private associations and sense impressions, of conversational tones, of social contexts.

His is a personal language in the sense that it expresses the emotions of a fallen human being who sees and shares the sufferings of all men. Yet in another sense it is an impersonal language with the impersonality of a natural force, of a bird-song rising from the dark recess of the "shadiest Covert." It has the power and compression of private prayer, yet it is addressed to all men, with the conviction that we will share the speaker's great concerns. It is a unique language because its reference is both historical and psychological, its application both universal and individual, its pitch heroic, its intensity lyrical, its tone a beautiful mingling of judgment and sympathy. Such a fusion of qualities is possible only to a narrator who is fallen but redeemed like the blind bard, a creature limited like the bird but capable of flight and endowed with the power of heavenly song. This tone expresses in the voice of the narrator Milton's vision of the inner life of every man in its eternal relation to nature, to history, and to God.

—Anne Davidson Ferry, *Milton's Epic Voice: The Narrator in Paradise Lost* (Cambridge, MA: Harvard University Press, 1967), pp. 179–81

LESLIE BRISMAN ON ADAM AND EVE AFTER THE FALL

[Leslie Brisman (b. 1944) is a professor of English at Yale University and the author of *Romantic Origins* (1978), *The Voice of Jacob: On the Composition of Genesis* (1990), and *Milton's Poetry of Choice and Its Romantic Heirs* (1973), from which the following extract is taken. Here, Brisman finds that Adam and Eve's wanderings after the Fall are representative of their freedom of choice and their entrance into historical time.]

For the reader the Fall is the great moment that Milton makes present, and subsequent history, like the memories of Adam and Eve before the Fall, leave little room for option. Alternatives are real when they are simultaneous, not sequential, but the vision of history seems involved in sequentiality, event following event in a pattern that would seem to be at least as remote from the will of Adam as the first steps of Eve are from her "innate" desires. One might compare the determination that Eve remembers—"with that thy gentle hand / Seiz'd mine"—with the sense that all is now determined in the last angelic act: "In either hand the hast'ning Angel caught / Our ling'ring Parents" (XII.637–638). Neither occasion seems to present much choice, and even the final image, "They hand in hand with wand'ring steps and slow, / Through *Eden* took thir solitary way," though it lets them take their time, does not seem to offer opportunity for alternative. Why not cry out, like Camus's hero, that alternatives "would come to absolutely the same thing. . . . To stay, or to make a move—it came to much the same"? If the choice is between staying in one particular place outside paradise or moving to another, how much choice is there? What matter if "The World was all before them, where to choose / Thir place of rest" when a flaming brand guards the entrance to paradise?

It is against such objections that *Paradise Lost* must reestablish the validity of alternative after the Fall. Every spatial image participates in the symbolic structure that makes the choice of "Thir place of rest" not an indifferent but a symbolic option. In his series of visions Michael makes physical stages into stages in a spiritual progress, and he turns from vision to prophecy as if from more immediate to more remote place. The physical stasis of "resting place" becomes emblematic of the temporal stasis which is the setting of choices, the moments of self-confrontation interposed between the going that is life and the ultimate arrest that Adam learns has been postponed:

> Death,
> Then due by sentence when thou didst transgress,
> Defeated of his seizure many days
> Giv'n thee of Grace.   [XI.252–255]

"Many days" are a period of choice during which man may repent; "Grace" makes existence in time a grace period between the Fall and the final judgment. Death, conceived when man fell but not brought into being immediately, shares in the two-stage creation that is as central to Miltonic theology as it is to human biology; existence in time becomes, not the penalty, but the "interposed ease" between necessitated and actualized finitude. Adam's great option is the option of seeing things thus, and stands as a model for the reader's great option so to view experience and find the justifications of God's ways in the adjustments of perspective toward them. Setting out into history, man is confronted with the choice of viewing historical sequence in the light that all events "rising or falling still advance his praise" (V.191).

Thus the sense of option at the end of the epic is not a vestigial remainder of the Fall but a new attitude toward fallen time. The immensity of one particular choice is replaced by the immensity of futurity; though there is not another tree of knowledge, there is the knowledge of subsequent history to be faced. Future time will provide repeated opportunities to test man, to create a pattern out of his repeated falls. But more important, futurity itself replaces the Fall; standing at the threshold of time replaces the experience of deciding for all time. It may be inadequate to speak of Adam and Eve "accepting" the yoke of wandering, for it is not a new choice they make that takes the place of the wrong choice they made. Adam's education does not involve making one more choice but rather, preparing for the conditions of a world of continual choice. Stevens says:

> He had to choose. But it was not a choice
> Between excluding things. It was not a choice
>
> Between, but of. He chose to include the things
> That in each other are included, the whole,
> The complicate, the amassing harmony.

The paradisal choice "between" is replaced with the choice "of" a world of complete, "amassing harmony"; the eternal presentness of paradise is replaced with the perpetual presentness of the fallen world which repeatedly presents man with lit-

tle crossroads, instantaneous options, the continual succession
of moments becoming past.
—Leslie Brisman, *Milton's Poetry of Choice and Its Romantic
Heirs*, (Ithaca, NY: Cornell University Press, 1973), pp. 169–72

CHRISTOPHER HILL ON MILTON AND THE ENGLISH CIVIL WAR

[Christopher Hill (b. 1912), who has taught at Balliol
College, Oxford (where he was Master in Modern
History), and Open University, is one of the most distinguished historians of our time. His works include
Change and Continuity in Seventeenth-Century England
(1974), *The Century of Revolution 1603–1714* (1980),
and *The Experience of Defeat: Milton and Some
Contemporaries* (1984). In this extract from *Milton and
the English Revolution* (1977), Hill detects significant
parallels between various incidents in *Paradise Lost* and
historical events during and after the English Civil War.]

The poem was no doubt planned as a whole before the
Restoration of May 1660. Nevertheless there must have been a
break in 1660, when Milton was in danger of his life and had to
go into hiding; and a further interruption when he was in
prison. It would have been dangerous for friends to visit his
hiding-place for the sole purpose of taking down from his dic-
tation, and impossible when he was imprisoned. The invocation to Book VII suggests a fresh start, under more difficult circumstances; the conjecture that Books I to VI were written (at
least in first draft) before the Restoration, Books VII to XII after
it, appears to be borne out by the evidence of style, which links
the last six books with *Paradise Regained* and *Samson
Agonistes* more closely than with the first six books. But 'I sing
. . . unchanged' may also be intended to recall to the fitter
audience for whom *Paradise Lost* was written the John Milton
whom they knew as the defender of divorce, regicide and
the republic.

There is a shift of emphasis in the last six books of the epic. Until April 1660 the revolutionaries still held power, however insecurely. The Royalists had been defeated, although they were desperately scheming revenge. In Books I and II Satan is wrong but grandly wrong. His attempt 'against the omnipotent to rise in arms' (VI. 136) seemed as absurd as a Royalist attempt to reverse the verdict of history. But after May 1660 Satan was not trying vainly to recover power in England: he had won it. His degradation in the second half of the epic is the greater because of Milton's disgusted realization of the power and influence of evil. It is paralleled by the stepping forward of the Creator-Son and the withdrawal of the impersonal Father. We should not then see Satan just as the apotheosis of rebellion. One subject of *Paradise Lost* is indeed rebellion, but Milton had himself been a rebel; he wanted now to know where he and his fellows had been mistaken, what kind of rebellion was justified and what not.

Satan, no less than Christ, is a king. His approach to Eve is a parody of courtly love at Henrietta Maria's court. Satan was 'by merit raised' to kingship in hell, as the Son had been in heaven. The analogy with the Son is stressed throughout. Sin, Death and Satan are the infernal Trinity: I see no reason why Milton should not parody this concept, in which he himself did not believe. In the early books Satan's 'grandeur' and 'ruined splendour' predominate. But Satan is also an Asiatic tyrant, associated with Turkish despotism (X.457)—as Charles I had been in *Eikonoklastes*. Since 1649 another group of men had been called Turkish bashaws—Cromwell's Major-Generals. It is not unlikely that there is something of them in the fallen angels. The latter are not mere personifications of evil. They were angels of light who have rejected the light. As Northrop Frye says, 'into Satan Milton has put all the horror and distress with which he contemplated the egocentric revolutionaries of his time', whose romantic rhetoric had got them—and those who trusted them—nowhere.

If, among other things, the character of Satan alludes to some of the ways in which the Good Old Cause had gone wrong, it is to be expected that he will contain a good deal of Milton, who recognized that he too was not without responsi-

bility for its failure. Milton's intellect now told him that he must accept God's will, if only because the Father is omnipotent: but his submission to the events of 1655–60 was highly reluctant. Satan, the battleground for Milton's quarrel with himself, saw God as arbitrary power and nothing else. Against this he revolted: the Christian, Milton knew, must accept it. Yet how could a free and rational individual accept what God had done to his servants in England? On this reading, Milton expressed through Satan (of whom he disapproved) the dissatisfaction which he felt with the Father (whom intellectually he accepted).
—Christopher Hill, *Milton and the English Revolution* (New York: Viking Press, 1977), pp. 365–67

MAUREEN QUILLIGAN ON GENDER ROLES IN *PARADISE LOST*

[Maureen Quilligan (b. 1944) is a professor of English at the University of Pennsylvania. She has written *The Language of Allegory* (1979) and *Milton's Spenser* (1983), from which the following extract is taken. Here, Quilligan observes that the subjugation of Eve to Adam in *Paradise Lost* denies her a direct relationship with God and, therefore, the power to challenge her husband.]

In ⟨. . .⟩ *Tetrachordon* Milton ⟨. . .⟩ went so far as to allow the woman to rule the man, if she were in fact his natural superior: for then "a superior and more natural law comes in, that the wiser should govern the less wise, whether male or female."

Against these startling and sweeping freedoms, Milton places the originary law:

> He for God only, she for God in him.

What is perhaps less immediately striking, but more profoundly interesting (in the context of Milton's sense of his inspiration) is that in this arrangement of the wife's subjection to her husband there is established not only a sexual hierarchy, but a mediated position for the woman with respect to the divine source. *It negates a direct relationship between God and woman.* She is "covered" by her husband, the male, and it is only through him that she may experience the divine. The purpose of her existence is to know divinity, but only mediately, through the darkened glass of her husband's divinity within.

The reasons for this choice (⟨George⟩ Fox at least had taken a different stand on Eve's status in paradise) are understandable in terms of the social history of seventeenth-century England. If each believer had become his own priest, and was no longer a member of an institutionally visible church, this priest found his congregation shrunk to the literal foundation upon which Paul had based his metaphoric description of Christ's relationship to his church: the love of a husband for his wife. The monarchial state had also dissolved, to be reconstituted anew but without the divine sanctions so successfully promulgated by Elizabeth and so unsuccessfully by the Stuarts. Radical Protestants were thrown back on the one social unit that might still stand—the nuclear family. The intense pressures on this unit required new political emphases, and the stress of the Puritan theology, while it looks like a fostering of woman's status, actually puts her—as Milton does—in a more mediated position. As Lawrence Stone points out, "one of the first results of the doctrine of holy matrimony was a strengthening of the authority of the husband over the wife, and an increased readiness of the latter to submit herself to the dictates of the former. . . . This is similar to the paradox by which the first result of an increased concern for children was a greater determination to crush their sinful wills by worshipping them."

Such is the chicken-and-egg problem of social change that it is also a distinct possibility that the need to reorient the family along stricter hierarchical lines was a cause of the doctrine of holy matrimony, not merely its result. Increasing the authority of the husband over the wife is a conservative social move designed to act as a safety valve on the revolutionary energies unleashed by the Reformation: if there were to be no more bishops and no more kings, there were still to be, finally and irrevocably, patriarchs. Smaller their kingdoms than before, but patriarchies nonetheless.

For a woman to have inspiration directly from God would be to threaten the last hierarchical relationship left; she would thereby have the authority to challenge her husband. By purging his audience of bacchantic revelers Milton purges the disordered unreason of anyone who would not be a fit reader. But taken in its Ovidian context, Milton is purging the maenad female reader who insists on a more direct relationship of her own to divine inspiration. This may seem needlessly to narrow the definition of the unfit—doubtless many more readers than frenzied Protestant prophetesses actually belong in that number. But it usefully indicates the place where Milton draws the line between his traditional, masculine poetic inspiration—at the end of a long line of both pagan and Hebrew prophets— and the newer enthusiasms in which women could legitimately participate (and for which Milton has some Protestant political sympathies). It distinguishes the works of inspiration—some are true vocations, others are not.

The casting out of the maenad reader also usefully suggests where Milton's female reader, reading as a female, must place herself. To be a fit reader, the woman must accept a mediated, covered position, must freely choose to conform to the hierarchy. The hierarchical arrangement is flatly stated; it is not something Milton argues. The arrangement holds by divine fiat (rather like "die he or justice must"); and to "justify" God's ways to woman is not to explain the situation, but to make her choose to accept it. The entire pressure of the argument of *Paradise Lost* as directed at this "covered" female reader is for her freely to choose the mediated position and to accept its rewards with gratitude. And the poem most persuasively holds that there are rewards, rewards as great, in fact, as the rewards held out for a man's acceptance of Christ to which they have from the time of Paul been an analogue. Adam chooses to die for love of Eve. Christ chooses to die for love of man. The first choice is wrong and the second is right: but they are both based in love. And one may heretically suspect that Adam's offered sacrifice derives from the divinity within him for which Eve was made.

—Maureen Quilligan, *Milton's Spenser: The Politics of Reading* (Ithaca, NY: Cornell University Press, 1983), pp. 224–26

BARBARA KIEFER LEWALSKI ON SATAN AND THE CLASSICAL HERO

[Barbara Kiefer Lewalski (b. 1931), the Alumni-Alumnae University Professor of English at Brown University, has written *Milton's Brief Epic* (1966), a celebrated study of *Paradise Regain'd*, as well as *Donne's Anniversaries and the Poetry of Praise* (1973) and *Protestant Poetics and the Seventeenth-Century Religious Epic* (1979). In this extract from her book on *Paradise Lost* (1985), Lewalski maintains that Milton derived the heroic image of Satan from classical epics, but in doing so he was expressing his own moral judgment of those epics.]

That Milton portrays Satan largely in terms of the heroic mode is a commonplace of criticism, as is the idea that the Satanic heroic is a debased version of the classical heroic ethos. Readers readily perceive that those parts of *Paradise Lost* concerned with Satan's activities are replete with epic matter and motivations, epic genre conventions, and constant allusions to specific passages in famous heroic poems, recalling thereby the glorious deeds, the heroic virtues, and the characteristic emotion—wonder—which Renaissance critics identified with these genres and these poems. Even so, we need to observe more precisely the very comprehensive range of heroic genres that Milton associates with Satan, including all the chief varieties of epic, romance, and heroic tragedy. And in doing so we need to examine just how he makes such links, and why.

Milton begins to develop the Satanic heroic mode in the opening books of *Paradise Lost* by associating with Satan generic topoi from one after another of the heroic genres. Also, by specific allusions to the *Iliad*, the *Odyssey*, the *Aeneid*, and other heroic poems, he identifies these poems as subtexts for the Satanic episodes. We are thereby alerted to attend to the generic paradigms which take shape gradually as the poem proceeds, and to trace the analogies to major heroic poems through the continuing verbal allusions, plot analogies, and references to scenes and motifs. The dynamics of the poem lead us to trace each of these patterns to its completion.

To develop the story of Satan, Milton invoked the generic paradigms and primary exemplars of the major epic and tragic kinds and their permutations, interweaving them and at the same time showing Satan's continued declination from higher to lower heroic kinds and models. Specifically, Satan's nature and role are analyzed through the debased, perverse, or parodic analogies they offer, first, to characters from the epic of strife and from the biblical "Exodus" epic; then from heroic tragedy; then from various forms of quest epic and romance; then from Ovid's *Metamorphoses*. This generic strategy is obviously addressed to an audience whose "fitness" is (in part at least) a function of their considerable literary experience and cultural sophistication.

Milton's intention is not to condemn classical epic or romance or tragedy, nor is it to exalt Satan as hero. Here as elsewhere literary genre is a vehicle of artistic imagination and of accommodation, making primordial evil comprehensible to poet and reader in all its attractiveness, complexity, multiplicity, and familiar local manifestations. Milton uses genre also for educative purposes: to lead readers to measure Satan against a great range of heroes and heroic actions, and against all these standards to find him wanting. We are to recognize—by degrees and through a process of comparison, contrast, and judgment—just what the Satanic heroism is, as we find that it involves the perversion of *all* heroic values that we have admired in literature and throughout history. At length, having redefined our concept of the heroic, we are asked to measure that concept against a divine standard of action and speech which incorporates but transforms and transcends the highest human heroism. ⟨. . .⟩

The Bard presents Satan and the fallen angels with reference to a wide range of generic paradigms and also specific patterns derived from major works in the heroic mode. Interweaving them, and at the same time ordering them so as to display Satan's decline, he defines a complex attitude toward the heroic in the literary tradition. We come to see that Satan and his crew pervert all the heroic values set forth in the greatest epics, romances, and tragedies we know. However, the fact that Satan is Achillean, or Promethean, or Odyssean, or

Ovidian, does not mean that Achilles, or Prometheus, or Odysseus, or Ovid, or the various romance heroes are Satanic. Those heroes, those values, those genres, and those works are not in themselves debased by the Satanic association. Rather, it is by measuring Satan against the heroic standards embodied in those works that we come to recognize how far Satan has perverted what in him was (and in some measure remains) magnificent.

Yet by the same process we become conscious of the inadequacy and fragility of all the heroic virtues celebrated in literature, of the susceptibility of them all to demonic perversion. The Bard's generic strategy leads us by stages to refine our concept of the heroic, pointing us at last toward the divine heroic model, which subsumes what is best in the various literary formulations of human heroism—and perfects it.
> —Barbara Kiefer Lewalski, *Paradise Lost and the Rhetoric of Literary Forms* (Princeton: Princeton University Press 1985), pp. 55–56, 77–78

JOHN M. STEADMAN ON SATAN AND ORATORY

[John M. Steadman (b. 1918) is a former professor of English at the University of California at Riverside. He has written several books on Milton, including *Milton and the Renaissance Hero* (1967), *Milton's Biblical and Classical Imagery* (1984), and *Moral Fiction in Milton and Spenser* (1995). In this extract, Steadman argues that Satan's chief means of persuading both himself and others of his heroic stature is the use of oratory in the manner of "wily Ulysses."]

The relationship between commentary and demonstration is, however, only one aspect of the problem of consistency in character. More fundamental is the alleged contrast between the "heroic" Satan of Books I and II and the "degraded" devil of the later books. A notorious example, in ⟨A. J. A.⟩ Waldock's opinion, is the disparity between Satan's opening addresses and his soliloquy in Book IV.

> O then at last relent: is there no place
> Left for Repentance, none for Pardon left?
> None left but by submission; and that word
> *Disdain* forbids me. (IV, 79–82)

In point of fact, the *ethos* explicit in this passage bears a striking resemblance to the character implicit in Satan's first address. (Indeed, there are verbal echoes, and these are not, apparently, accidental.) Here are the same refusal to repent and the same disdain, though arrayed in less sumptuous oratory than before. The soliloquy voices the same despair as the earlier oration and exhibits the same characteristic *ethos* of the reprobate.

The alleged contradiction between the heroic and degraded Satans is essentially an illusion. In one sense Satan is already degraded from the moment he first makes his appearance, even though he does his best to disguise the fact from his fellows and from himself. His fall is itself a visible and tangible sign of his degradation in more than one respect: political and moral, physical and metaphysical. Perhaps the most remarkable feature of the first two books is the skill with which Satan and his fellows seek to persuade themselves, and one another, that their degradation is a triumph and their humiliation an exaltation. Certainly, they have succeeded in persuading more than one critic, dizzied by Satan's "bad eminence" and dazzled by the barbaric glitter of his throne. Waldock was not alone in failing to recognize that the Satan of the first two books is essentially and fundamentally degraded and that much of the power and beauty of the opening results from the devil's attempt to mask the fact of his degradation from himself and from his companions.

The degraded Satan of the later books is by no means a contemptible figure. He is still a heroic image, albeit falsely heroic. Even in his bestial disguises he bears a significant resemblance to heroic prototypes, though this time his affinities are less with Achilles and Agamemnon than with the crafty Ithacan, *polytropos* Odysseus. His tongue proves more lethal than his gunpowder, and the masterly oration whereby he seduces Eve would do credit even to the wily Ulysses. Indeed the question of his heroism is closely associated with the problem of his rhetorical skill. Besides the deceptive eloquence that prevails on Eve and links him with Odysseus, the stirring harangues that kindle new spirit in his defeated legions associate him with Aeneas, Agamemnon, and other heroes of the Greco-Trojan cycle. Even more significant, however, is the classical ideal of the hero as orator. In the *Cratylus,* Plato had suggested a derivation of *heros* from *eirein* ("to speak") and interpreted the ancient heroes as "a race of orators and sophists." This suggestion was echoed by Renaissance authors, such as Charles Estienne and Torquato Tasso. For many Renaissance readers, moreover, this conception of the orator as hero would have been reinforced by Cicero's quasi-heroic treatment of the rhetorician in his *De Oratore.*

In *Paradise Lost,* Satan conquers a world not by martial force (like the conventional epic hero) but by verbal persuasion. In this respect he resembles the heroes whom Plato had described as "rhetorōn kai sophistōn genos." And, indeed, in the crucial temptation scene Milton explicitly compares him to

> som Orator renound
> In *Athens* or free *Rome,* where Eloquence
> Flourished. (IX, 670–72)

Against the background of this tradition the portrait of Satan as orator—as rhetorician and as sophist—is just as heroic as the earlier portrait of Satan as martial combatant. Milton has not violated the consistency of his heroic *eidolon* in depicting Satan's alteration from vainglorious warrior to smooth-tongued rhetorician. The archangel still reflects a conventional conception of heroism, which long abuse had generally rendered vicious.

—John M. Steadman, *Milton and the Paradoxes of Renaissance Heroism* (Baton Rouge: Louisiana State University Press, 1987), pp. 117–19

❖

[Catherine Belsey (b. 1940), lecturer in English at University College in Cardiff, Wales, is the author of *Critical Practice* (1980), *The Subject of Tragedy* (1985), and *Desire: Love Stories in Western Culture* (1994). In this extract from her book on Milton (1988), Belsey argues that *Paradise Lost* need not be read exclusively as the viciously antifeminist text it has generally been taken to be.]

The feminist critique of *Paradise Lost* goes back at least to Charlotte Brontë's *Shirley*. Its history is traced by Sandra Gilbert and Susan Gubar in *The Madwoman in the Attic,* where Milton is identified as the aesthetic patriarch a series of women writers have had to overthrow in the anxiety of anti-feminist influence. None the less, there are recent instances of feminist appropriation in *Paradise Lost,* and I want to contribute to this process of rereading, on the basis that the text can be seen at certain points to exceed the utterances of its own narrative voice. If *Paradise Lost* is not a feminist text—and it certainly isn't—it can still, I believe, be read on behalf of feminism. And Graves's novel ⟨*The Story of Marie Powell: Wife to Mr. Milton,* 1943⟩, more subtle and more incisive than the official literary criticism of its period, helps perhaps in spite of itself, to illuminate what is dark in Milton's epic. ⟨. . .⟩

Paradise Lost is an epic poem, but the central figures of the emerging humanist text are beginning also to be identifiable as characters in a novel. Though their individuality tends to be masked by the epic voice they all share with the narrator, the text includes what seem to be moments of pure *vraisemblance,* when their speech or behaviour can be read as expressive of an idiosyncratic interiority. At such moments the figures appear endowed with a life which exceeds their representative epic status. If this is true of Eve, it is possible to see how Graves, reading the epic as narrative fiction, might find in Eve the basis of the novelistic character he attributes to Marie. Both Eve and Marie have golden hair which reaches to their waists (IV, 304–5). Both are outspoken, though capable of self-control. Both, of course, defend their freedom. Is Eve also witty?

It seems unlikely that Eve would be permitted to make a joke. Epics are no laughing matter. And yet the behaviour of the newly created Eve, read as if it were an episode in a novel, at once presents itself as comedy. Drawn to look into the lake, she sees an image which bends to meet her:

> I started back,
> It started back, but pleased I soon returned,
> Pleased it returned as soon with answering looks   (IV, 462–64)

Moments later she sees Adam for the first time. This image is far less agreeable than the one in the lake. Again she starts back—until Adam persuades her to return and recognize his superior 'manly grace' (IV, 490). The account of Eve surveying Adam, finding him unappealing and turning back resolutely to her lake-mirror is an unexpected twist in the story which is pure delight. The comedy depends on the symmetry between the two events: each time she looks, starts back, returns to the image. It also depends on our knowing what the new-born Eve does not: that lakes are looking-glasses, that men are sexy in a *different* way. And yet it is Eve who retrospectively recounts all this to Adam, deliberately drawing attention to her own ingenuousness in a piece of innocent sexual teasing which places her as simultaneously knowing and naive. Adam smiles at her story (IV, 499). And so, perhaps, when he read it, did Robert Graves, who unconsciously found in the work of the poet he denounced the character of the heroine his novel offers for our admiration.

The advent of humanism and the novel, like the redefinition of marriage as a partnership, did not, however, spell the dissolution of patriarchal relations, but only their rearrangement. Women were still the *opposite* sex, everything that was not masculine. If the moment of sexual differentiation allows Eve a voice, it is none the less precisely a *differentiated* voice, charming, erotic, experiential. Adam smiles 'with superior love' (IV, 499) as his bride makes winning comedy out of her own artlessness. When Adam records the same incident it is not comic, but moralized and theorized, and the voice is rational, analytical, and masculine. Eve's hesitation is now defined as the effect of

innocence and virgin modesty,
Her virtue and the conscience of her worth
That would be wooed, and not unsought be won.   (VIII, 501–3)

—Catherine Belsey, *John Milton: Language, Gender, Power*
(Oxford: Basil Blackwell, 1988), pp. 59–62

DAVID LOEWENSTEIN ON MICHAEL'S PROPHECY

[David Loewenstein, a professor of English at the University of Wisconsin, has written a monograph on *Paradise Lost* (1993) and coedited *Politics, Poetics, and Hermeneutics in Milton's Prose* (1990). In this extract from *Milton and the Drama of History* (1990), Loewenstein focuses on Michael's prophecy of human history in book eleven of *Paradise Lost,* which echoes Milton's own views on the causes of political and ecclesiastical conflict in his own time.]

Milton's interest in probing history to reveal the causes of national and ecclesiastical failure was, we have seen earlier in this study, already manifested in his first polemical work. The historical discourse in *Of Reformation* moved from the age of Wyclif to the discord of his own times, with numerous references to the tragic consequences of the Donation of Constantine. Registering a tension between competing visions of millennial renovation and national regression, the historical sections of Milton's tract revealed that, while "the very essence of Truth" might be "plainnesse, and brightnes," the "darknes and crookednesse" of history was indeed of our own making. His *History of Britain* probed even further into national history, going all the way back to Britain's legendary beginnings. This massive project disclosed a labyrinthine process of history in which the nation seemed to go through a series of falls and cycles—"the Revolution of like Calamities" was the phrase Milton used to describe them—preventing it from making genuine progress and perhaps even leading the frustrated poetic historiographer to abort his weary account at the time of the Norman Conquest. And so by asking in *Paradise Lost* "what cause / Mov'd our Grand Parents in that happy State . . . to fall off / From thir Creator" (I.28–31) the poet takes his historical inquiry all the way back to the very beginning of human history. As recent critics have noted, *Paradise Lost* is a poem deeply concerned with the origins and causes of spiritual and physical events alike. Here I would stress that the poet's historiographical enterprise in the concluding books of the poem specifically recalls his search for historical causes and explanations in the revolutionary prose works. "The CAUSES that hitherto have hindred" reformation in his own age, to invoke the subtitle of Milton's very first polemical exploration into the past, would now be understood most truthfully in his epic by dramatizing that original "cause" and envisioning the whole uneven course of human history from Adam to the Apocalypse.

Michael's prophesy in *Paradise Lost,* then, constitutes Milton's most ambitious attempt to confront and examine those causes which had led to the turbulent course of ecclesiastical and political history throughout the ages, and which hindered, as he says in his first polemic, "the forwarding of *true Discipline.*" The drama of national historic destiny, a major concern of the revolutionary prose works, is now situated in the context of the full spectacle of tragic human history which Michael unfolds before Adam. Likewise, the prose writer's aim to instruct his nation in the relapses of history and the means of social renovation is refocused in Milton's poem in terms of Michael's task to instruct Adam in the nature of historical truth and the revelation of God's Word in future ages. We may recall that the prose work explicitly devoted to "repair[ing] the ruins of our first parents by regaining to know God aright" begins with Milton addressing Hartlib thus: "I shall . . . strait conduct ye to a hill side, where I will point ye out the right path of a vertuous and noble Education; laborious indeed at the first ascent, but else so smooth, so green, so full of goodly prospect" (*Of Education*). Similarly, Michael begins Adam's laborious re-education after the Fall by conducting him up "a Hill / Of Paradise" where they "ascend / In the Visions of God," so that Adam beholds a "prospect" of history (though not one that is particularly "goodly") with its succession of evil ages (XI.376–78, 380). Milton takes one of the more conventional functions of history in the Renaissance—namely, to instruct—and reinvests it with new significance and intensity. Adam's education in history will enable him to experience and understand the "darkness and crookednesse" which has ensued from that first historical pattern of call, disobedience, and exile. Nor will history in his case serve, as it so often did in Milton's age, as a refuge from devouring time. Rather for Adam and his race, these trying history lessons mean a painful immersion into time and mortality.

Much like Augustine in the *City of God,* Milton depicts postlapsarian history in terms of ongoing conflict and opposition. According to Augustine, human society is rooted in a disordered *saeculum* brought about by a conflict between the *civitas terrena* and the *civitas Dei,* one representing the values of unbelief, the other representing the values of faith. The whole course of human history—past, present, and future—essentially dramatizes this powerful tension of forces. Rooted in conflict and strife, human society and its history can expect no redemption, except eschatologically. The history of fallen man, both Augustine and Milton would agree, is characterized by wandering, mutability, and disorder, though Milton does indeed vividly imagine the positive dynamics of "ceaseless change" (V.183) in prelapsarian Eden, as well as heaven's own "Grateful vicissitude" (VI.8; cf. V.629). Like Augustine's work, the vision of history in *Paradise Lost* projects a sense of the dramatic conflict in the postlapsarian world—where "supernal Grace" must contend with "sinfulness of Men" (XI.359–60)—beginning with the strife between Cain and Abel, and continuing throughout world history. As Augustine observes, "the conflict between Cain and Abel displayed the hostility between the two cities themselves, the City of God and the city of men."
—David Loewenstein, *Milton and the Drama of History* (Cambridge: Cambridge University Press, 1990), pp. 94–96

[John Reichert (b. 1935) is the author of *Making Sense of Literature* (1977) and *Milton's Wisdom* (1992), a book on *Paradise Lost* from which the following extract is taken. Here, Reichert discusses a variety of structural patterns in Milton's epic poem, based chiefly on the distinction between nature and Scripture.]

When Milton built the grand Palladian temple that is *Paradise Lost*, to what extent did he have in mind as structural principles the pair of books that we have been exploring? I am persuaded that in fact he may have had them very much in mind. The structure that emerges, as will be clear, is not one that the reader is likely to be aware of while caught up in the process of reading the poem. It involves a symmetrical arrangement of the whole epic, an arrangement one can perceive only after stepping back from the text to reflect on how its parts are ordered. For the reader carried along by the ongoing movement of a phrase or sentence or episode, it remains as unnoticed as the regularity that governs that "mystical dance" in heaven: "mazes intricate, / Eccentric, intervolved, yet regular / Then most, when most irregular they seem" (5.620–24). One feels the intricacies, the intervolutions, as one reads. Yet the regularity is present, and its features coincide with the most familiar turning points of the poem, such as the prologues to Books 3 and 7, the poet's assertion that "half yet remains unsung" (7.21), and Michael's pausing "betwixt the world destroyed and world restored" at the beginning of Book 12.

Let me suggest, then, saving many of the details for subsequent chapters, that the central eight books of the poem, Books 3 through 10, would appear to turn, at their midpoint, and at the midpoint of the epic, from a preoccupation with nature to a preoccupation with the Word. The invocation to Book 3, which has at its core the fact that for the blind Milton the book of nature's works has been "expunged and razed," is addressed to "holy Light" and treats of eyes and "mortal sight," of physical blindness and inner vision. Here Milton is the poet as seer, and the invocation concludes with a prayer for the purgation and dispersal of "all mists" from his mind so that he may "see and tell / Of things invisible to mortal sight." In Book 3 the emphasis is on the Son as obedient to, and expressive of, God's face. He is the "radiant image" of his father (3.63). Books 3 through 6, in keeping with this beginning, have as their dominant motif the seeing and reading of nature's works, concluding, in Book 6, with a scene depicting their destruction.

The invocation to Book 7, though strikingly similar in its structure to the invocation to Book 3, has at its core not Milton's blindness and inner vision, but his profound dependence on Urania's "voice divine" to guide his song. It treats of Urania's and Wisdom's "celestial song," of the hoarseness and muteness which could silence the poet's own "mortal voice," and of the "evil tongues," "barbarous dissonance," and "savage clamor" that threaten to drown it out. Here Milton is the poet as singer, and he prays, "Still govern thou my song, / Urania, and fit audience find." In Book 7 the emphasis is on the Son as expressing not the face but the Word of God—his voice—and on the obedience of both Chaos and the creatures to that voice. Put differently, here Adam and Eve are not seeing and reading nature's works. They are listening to Raphael's voice and hearing in it also God's creating words. Recurring fourteen times through its pages, the refrain of Book 7 is the simple but powerful fiat, the creative performative "let there be" or "let the. . . ." The dominant motif of Books 7 through 10 is the Word: first in its issuing forth to create the world; next in Adam's instruction under the tutelage of the Word; then in Satan's successful replacing of it with his own words; and finally, in Book 10, in Adam and Eve's collaborative and ultimately saving meditation on the Word that leads them to turn to God for forgiveness.

A similar movement from creatures to the Word, or from the visual to the audible, can be seen in Books 11 and 12, as Michael restores Adam's understanding, first by teaching him to see and interpret the misshapen creatures of the fallen world, and then by teaching him to listen to, to understand, and to speak, the words of Scripture. The sins or vices portrayed in Book 11 are directed against the creatures. They are sins of brute violence and gross, self-destructive intemperance:

the murder of Abel; the hideous diseases of the lazarhouse brought about by the perversion of "pure nature's healthful rules" (11.523); the godly-seeming men who, "unmindful of their maker . . . yield up all their virtue" to the "lustful appetance" of the "fair atheists" (11.611–25); the destruction of the creatures of the pastoral world as seen in the slaughter of cattle, oxen, ewes, and lambs, followed immediately by the destruction of a city and the massacre of its inhabitants (11.646–82); and finally, the luxury, riot, prostitution, rape, adultery, and "civil broils" (11.714–18) that lead God to repent himself "of man depraved" and bring on the Flood. Book 11 ends, at last, with the saving of the creatures as they enter Noah's ark in "sevens and pairs," and with the rainbow signaling God's intention to let his creation survive.

Book 12, on the other hand, is concerned almost entirely with the corruption and preservation of language as represented in both the spoken and written word. Michael tells Adam of Babel and Pentecost, of promises, covenants, and laws—of the preserving of the "records" of the covenant in the ark (12.252), of the "written records pure" left by Jesus' followers (12.513), of the Spirit engraving the law of faith in the hearts of believers. Above all, its subject is Michael's gradual unfolding of the proto-covenant, the Word pronounced against the serpent, the meaning of which Adam and Eve had earlier, with considerable though incomplete success, struggled to understand.

The turn from Book 11 to Book 12 following the Flood parallels the transition from Book 6 to Book 7 following the picture of the destruction of the creatures in the war in heaven. Each picture of ruin is followed by a new beginning, the "world destroyed" followed by the "world restored" (12.3). Milton highlights the structural similarity. Metaphorically at the end of Book 6, and literally at the end of 11, evil is "soon / Driven back redounded as a flood on those / From whom it sprung" (7.56–58).

If one were to extrapolate from such evidence an overarching pattern, a schematic ordering of the twelve books of the poem, *Paradise Lost* would appear to be divided into three groups—Books 1 and 2, Books 3 through 10, and Books 11

and 12—with the first half of each group emphasizing nature, or the visual, and the second half Scripture, or the aural.
—John Reichert, *Milton's Wisdom: Nature and Scripture in Paradise Lost* (Ann Arbor: University of Michigan Press, 1992), pp. 51–53

ARNOLD STEIN ON MILTON AND DEATH

[Arnold Stein (b. 1915), a former professor at the University of Washington, Johns Hopkins University, and the University of Illinois, is the author of several volumes, including *Heroic Knowledge: An Interpretation of* Paradise Regained *and* Samson Agonistes (1957), *The Art of Presence: The Poet and* Paradise Lost (1977), and *The House of Death: Messages from the English Renaissance* (1986). In this extract, Stein studies the many forms of death in *Paradise Lost,* especially in Michael's lecture to Adam concerning the future of humanity.]

As the angel Michael begins the educational retraining that will prepare Adam to live in the world outside, the main purposes named to Adam are these: "to learn / True patience" (XI, 360–61), "to temper" extremes and bear contrary states:

> Prosperous or adverse: so shalt thou lead
> Safest thy life, and best prepared endure
> Thy mortal passage when it comes. (XI, 364–66)

Training for the new life is directed toward the new end of life, enduring "Thy mortal passage when it comes." Nothing in the course description leads one to expect easy pleasure, or to fill relaxed moments by contemplating the prospect of graduation. Some unhurried preliminaries have already taken place, and Michael has been "mild" and "benign" in answering Eve and Adam. Now Adam learns in an aside that a special kind of sleep has been arranged for Eve; he then is furnished with a brief vision of the future Kingdoms of the world, after which his eyesight is purged and he is directed to behold "Th'effects which thy original crime hath wrought" (XI, 424). This is the death of Abel, which begins as pastoral and ends as something else. When we witness the first human death in the world, and through the eyes of the father-to-be, whose responses to the sight are still governed by his having lived almost all his life in the state of innocence, we see an Adam deeply troubled but only half understanding the violence and apparent injustice. He cries out:

> O Teacher, some great mischief hath befall'n
> To that meek man, who well had sacrificed;
> Is piety thus and pure devotion paid? (XI, 450–52)

Though "also moved," like Adam and like us, the angel explains the incident in a calm manner and assures Adam that justice will be done.

In spite of the dismaying prospect of unborn sons murdering and dying, the central shock to Adam is the personal discovery:

> But have I now seen Death? Is this the way
> I must return to native dust? O sight
> Of terror, foul and ugly to behold,
> Horrid to think, how horrible to feel! (XI, 462–65)

Though Michael has explained that there will be revenge and reward, it is the death itself that grips Adam's attention, that and the instant imaginative transference to seeing, thinking, and feeling his own death. In this Adam anticipates Raleigh's insight and responds at once to the "counsell of Death." To move Adam from his demonstrated human base of terror and revulsion, Michael, though clearly working against a set time, needs to order and apply his lessons gradually. He chooses, first, to acknowledge but limit the terror and, second, to discipline the revulsion by repeating the basic experience through significantly progressing variations of the "foul and ugly." He begins by reminding Adam that he has thus far observed only death's "first shape on man." There are many shapes:

> and many are the ways that lead
> To his grim cave, all dismal; yet to sense
> More terrible at th'entrance than within.   (XI, 468–70)

Michael has the intuitive equipment of a master diplomat. He admits the undeniable truth at once: the cave is "grim" and all the ways to it are "dismal." But it is worse at the entrance than within. That piece of half-information may be worth something later. Besides, judgment is now limited to the report of sense and the difference between "More terrible at th'entrance" and less terrible "within." This leaves room for reports from the higher faculties contributing to judgment, and anticipates a more propitious time when the more fully informed listener may be ready to respond to a whole situation.

⟨. . .⟩ Before the first harsh lessons regarding death, Michael had encouraged Adam by announcing that his prayers had been heard and his death postponed. There would be time for him to repent and time for good deeds to cover the one bad act. Then just before he announced their banishment from Eden, Michael mentioned a new possibility: "well may then thy Lord appeased / Redeem thee quite from Death's rapacious claim" (XI, 257–58). This is a latent truth which will be brought forward again, somewhat further forward, advanced by being more definite, like a picture of improved clarity. The truth will finally be understood by Adam himself, who will participate in the revelation as his personal path of education converges with the working of typology. But not yet. The lament that immediately follows the news of banishment leaves the news of possible rescue from death unremarked, as if it were not heard or were less important than the threat of eviction. As a result, the possibility of rescue has no discernible effect on Michael's teaching and Adam's learning the rigid facts of death. The timing of Michael's optimistic suggestion belongs to the marvelous rationality of narrative and dramatic cooperating with a kind of theological vision that exceeds the rational. The signal of hope that is passed by now will emerge in a later fulfillment.

After his death Jesus will rise: "Thy ransom paid, which man from Death redeems" (XII, 424). Adam's own life and the judgment of death upon him are not for certain directly and fully

involved here but are, to some degree, related to the prophe-
sied redemption. A few lines later, however, the mention of
"temporal death" adds a degree of clarification that would
include Adam, or—not to be hasty in greeting the emergence
of typological significances—Adam could infer his potential eli-
gibility to join those whom Christ redeems from "a death like
sleep, / A gentle wafting to immortal life" (XII, 434–35).

The educational path that we may recognize as being largely
secular, continuous, and rational has been carefully followed
and honored. The basic method is an open one, that of dialogue. Its capacity for promoting personal growth is represented by Adam's increased participation in the dialogue. His
questions and responses improve greatly. On his own initiative
he acknowledges his Redeemer and declares himself "Taught
. . . by his example" that death is "to the faithful . . . the gate of
life" (XII, 572, 571). The emotions that rise in Adam and corre-
spond to both parts of his educational experience are those of
joy and love.

At the heart of Milton's process is a standard Renaissance
agreement concerning Christian death. The inherent fear of
death could best be answered and removed by an opposing
deep emotion, the love of God. There were well-known ways
of assisting and easing that process, but for Adam, the pioneer,
all the problems of his progress were unique. As we have
seen, Michael first prepared his student in a hundred lines; and
then, some eight hundred lines later, with no direct mention
made, the fear is gone. One imagines that many of Milton's
early readers would have recognized and enjoyed the play of
similarity and difference between their own modern practices
and the tutoring Adam received when he still had some nine
hundred years to live but was nevertheless obliged to follow an
immensely accelerated and packed schedule of learning.

At the very end of the poem Adam walks away from his past
and the irretrievable part of his loss, "with wand'ring steps and
slow," but with some restoration of optimism and with
Providence as his guide and the world "all before them, where
to choose"; yet this is a world that in his preview scrambled
after joy and was pursued by sorrow. Nevertheless, when
Adam walks away he is walking hand in hand with the woman

who will share his life and who, like himself, is almost as good
as new yet also worse and better.
—Arnold Stein, "Imagining Death: The Ways of Milton," *Milton
Studies* 29 (1992): 115–16, 119–20

DAVID REID ON THE TREE OF KNOWLEDGE

[David Reid (b. 1940) is a lecturer in English at the
University of Stirling in Scotland. He has edited *The
Party-Coloured Mind: Prose Relating to the Conflict of
Church and State in Seventeenth Century Scotland*
(1982) and has written *The Humanism of Milton's
Paradise Lost* (1993), from which the following extract
is taken. Here, Reid discusses the moral and theological
issues surrounding Adam and Eve's sampling of the
fruit of the Tree of Knowledge.]

Milton's treatment of free choice in Paradise can sound very
paradoxical. Adam and Eve were made sinless and naturally
good. The fall of such unflawed creatures makes everything
turn on the freedom of the will. The choice of evil cannot go
back to flaws in their nature, or their creator would be to
blame. So, evil must originate in the wills that choose. What
Milton shows, therefore, lies at the furthest extreme from what
Strindberg shows in *Miss Julie,* where the characters are compelled (and fascinated, one might say, since they watch themselves as in a dream) by murky motives. In *Paradise Lost,* the
motives are the arguments that are put to Adam and Eve, first
by Satan and then by themselves. They can be chosen or rejected rationally. The courses of action which Adam and Eve take
lie within their own powers. If in the end there is something
unaccountable about their choices of error, that is perhaps
because error is a lapse of mind and, like nonsense, cannot be
understood. Nevertheless, the lapse of mind hides behind a
show of rational deliberation, and the irrationality that is let in
with it does not implicate the unfallen natures of Adam and
Eve; it runs forwards into their future, not back into their past.

Yet, however, paradoxical an action caused by choice rather than motive may sound, it makes good human sense, if we get close to what Milton shows. First, though, we should consider the moral framework in which the choice of error is made. I shall not attempt a philosophical unraveling of the paradoxes involved, since I am not a philosopher and have not found that philosophical criticism unfolds the poem sensitively. I shall aim simply at some descriptive observations to show how Milton's treatment of free fall comes within the scope of moral understanding.

Milton has set up things morally so that Adam and Eve are faced with an absolute choice, by which they stand or fall. Perhaps even more than with Satan, it is hard to feel with them that the choice turns on an issue of life and death. God's prohibition stamps the fruit of the tree of knowledge as a symbol of obedience. To take the fruit is to violate the symbol and throw off the obedience. So much is clear; but, because the command bears the stamp of arbitrariness, we cannot feel that the issues of good and evil depend on it absolutely. It is not the absoluteness of the command that puts it outside natural moral comprehension. We feel immediately that the murders of Duncan and Desdemona are absolutely wrong. God's prohibition of the fruit, however, does not externalize a natural abhorrence. On the contrary, the prohibition sets up a duty entirely separate from human nature. By nature, Adam and Eve are neither inclined nor declined to what it orders. That leaves them free to obey without either natural compulsion or unnatural abstinence. They obey, rationally conscious that the fruit is a 'pledge of [their] obedience' (III, 95). It clearly matters to Milton that they should understand what is involved. He does not set out to show tragic choice stirring up emotional depths as Shakespeare does. He aims at clear representation of the rational will in its choice of irrationality and evil; but what he gains in clarity he loses in the command of an instinctive sense of good and evil.

The clarity of Milton's picture depends on a final arbitrariness, as he himself recognized in his *Christian Doctrine*. A command with moral reasons behind it would not serve. Adam and Eve do not need to be told, for instance, to love each other. They do so according to the free play of their natures. If, however, they enjoyed only that freedom from constraint, they would differ only in degree from the other animals; they would be God's toys. To bring about the freedom of free obedience, God has to make an arbitrary cut in things with the prohibition of the fruit, and in doing so makes Adam and Eve accountable beings. None of this, however, circumvents the arbitrariness of the prohibition, which we have had to take as a given. Once we do, we are free to see the Fall as a human action. Breakings of a divine and moral law involve the same emotions of the will. The error, guilt and repentance of Adam and Eve take a human course, and Milton's peculiar grasp of volition is as good moral psychology as religious psychology.

The other part of the moral framework to be clarified is freedom of choice. Milton's scheme of images, as we saw in the last chapter, makes up a hinged universe which turns on the freedom of the will. That points us in a useful direction. When thinking about free choice, it is better to look for alternative possibilities, a forking of ways in the situation itself, than to think only of some inherently indeterminate faculty within the characters themselves. The hinged universe, however, which leaves open the possibility of falling out of creation, is more of an epic metaphor for free choice than an actual moral situation that faces the characters with alternatives. What really sets up the terms of freedom is the prohibition itself, the final command or setting of limits to things that completes creation by conferring the reason that is also choice on human beings.

It seems highly puzzling that a prohibition should set free, that the blocking of a course of action with a command should somehow open up the world morally. I cannot satisfactorily unriddle all that is implied by the paradox, but certain things are clear. The prohibition makes a mark in the undifferentiated goodness of unfallen creation, the enormous bliss of the garden, in such a way that evil becomes a possibility. Adam and Eve consequently know what evil is as a possibility; they have an innocent knowledge, unlike the guilty knowledge of good and evil which they obtain by eating the fruit. Until the possibility is realized, it resolves itself without constraint simply as part of the freedom of innocence. It is a sort of shadow of the goodness of Paradise assuring us that the goodness stands in a three-dimensional moral world. Again, the prohibition implies freedom because it binds Adam and Eve in words. It is in the nature of power, however arbitrary, that where it imposes itself in words, in a command, it leaves one free to obey or disobey according to the discourse of one's reason. Finally, the prohibition determines innocence and guilt: innocence is obedience, guilt transgression. This explains the instantaneous fall. Formally, Adam and Eve are innocent until they decide to infringe the prohibition.

The way in which the prohibition distinguishes innocence and guilt should discourage us from looking at the passage from one state to the other metaphysically. It may perhaps substitute a legal fiction for a metaphysical puzzle, but it works in ways that make human sense. It clears up at least two unnecessary puzzles. First, since innocence means honouring the prohibition, we need not imagine something somehow sinful before the Fall about the paradisaical strayings of Adam and Eve, which indeed, if they were sinful, 'were to make Sinne of being a man'. Just because the prohibition lays down right and wrong so categorically, for 'the rest', as Eve says (IX, 653–4), they 'live / Law to ourselves', free of guilt and conscientious fears. Second, there is no need to be mystified by the corruption of the will immediately succeeding the eating of the fruit. Eve and Adam know what they have done, and their guilty knowledge of transgression fills them with crooked desires and fears. What corrupts them is a bad conscience.

—David Reid, *The Humanism of Milton's* Paradise Lost (Edinburgh: Edinburgh University Press, 1993), pp. 128–30

Books by
John Milton

A Maske Presented at Ludlow Castle, 1634 ⟨*Comus*⟩. 1637.

Epitaphium Damonis. c. 1640.

Animadversions upon the Remonstrants Defence, against Smectymnuus. 1641.

Of Prelatical Episcopacy, and Whether It May Be Deduc'd from the Apostolical Times. 1641.

Of Reformation: Touching Church-Discipline in England, and the Causes That Hitherto Have Hindered It. 1641.

An Apology against a Pamphlet Called A Modest Confutation of the Animadversions upon the Remonstrant against Smectymnuus. 1642.

The Reason of Church-Government Urg'd against Prelaty. 1642.

The Doctrine and Discipline of Divorce. 1643.

Areopagitica: A Speech for the Liberty of Unlicenc'd Printing. 1644.

The Judgment of Martin Bucer, concerning Divorce (translator). 1644.

Of Education. 1644.

Colasterion: A Reply to a Nameless Answer against The Doctrine and Discipline of Divorce. 1645.

Poems, Both English and Latin. 1645.

Tetrachordon: Expositions upon the Foure Chief Places in Scripture. 1645. *Eikonoklastes: In Answer to a Book Intitul'd* Eikon Basilike. 1649.

The Tenure of Kings and Magistrates. 1649.

Pro Populo Anglicano Defensio. 1651.

Pro Populo Anglicano Defensio Secunda. 1654.

Pro Se Defensio contra Alexandrum Morum. 1655.

The Cabinet-Council. 1658.

Considerations Touching the Likeliest Means to Remove Hirelings out of the Church. 1659.

A Treatise of Civil Power in Ecclesiastical Causes. 1659.

Brief Notes upon a Late Sermon, Titl'd, The Fear of God and the King by Matthew Griffith. 1660.

The Readie & Easy Way to Establish a Free Commonwealth. 1660.

Paradise Lost. 1667, 1674.

Accedence Commenc't Grammar. 1669.

The History of Britain. 1670.

Paradise Regain'd; to Which Is Added Samson Agonistes. 1671.

Artis Logicae Plenior Institutio. 1672.

Of True Religion, Haeresie, Schism, Toleration, and What Best Means May Be Us'd against the Growth of Popery. 1673.

Poems, &c., upon Several Occasions. 1673.

A Declaration. 1674.

Epistolarum Familiarum Liber Unus. 1674.

Literae Pseudo-Senatûs Anglicani. 1676.

Character of the Long Parliament. 1681.

A Brief History of Moscovia. 1682.

Republican-Letters. 1682.

Letters of State, from the Year 1649 till the Year 1659. 1694.

Poetical Works. Ed. Patrick Hume. 1695.

Works. 1697.

A Complete Collection of the Historical, Political, and Miscellaneous Works of John Milton. Ed. John Toland. 1698. 3 vols.

Poetical Works. 1707. 2 vols.

Original Letters and Papers of State Addressed to Oliver Cromwell. Ed. John Nickolls. 1743.

Prose Works. Ed. Charles Symmons. 1806. 7 vols.

De Doctrina Christiana Libri Duo. Ed. Charles Richard Sumner. 1825.

Poetical Works. Ed. John Mitford. 1832. 3 vols.

Works in Verse and Prose. Ed. John Mitford. 1851. 8 vols.

Poetical Works. Ed. George Gilfillan. 1853. 2 vols.

Poetical Works. Ed. David Masson. 1874. 3 vols.

A Common-place Book. Ed. A. J. Horwood. 1876.

Sonnets. Ed. Mark Pattison. 1883.

Poetical Works. Ed. H. C. Beeching. 1900.

Poetical Works. Ed. William Aldis Wright. 1903.

Poems. Ed. Herbert J. C. Grierson. 1925. 2 vols.

Works. Ed. Frank Allen Patterson et al. 1931–38. 18 vols. in 21.

Private Correspondence and Academic Exercises. Ed. and tr. Phyllis B. Tillyard and E. M. W. Tillyard. 1932.

Poetical Works. Ed. Helen Darbishire. 1952–55. 2 vols.

Complete Prose Works. Ed. Don M. Wolfe et al. 1953–82. 8 vols.

The Cambridge Milton. Ed. John Broadbent et al. 1972– .

The Macmillan Milton. Ed. C. A. Patrides et al. 1972– .

Works about
John Milton and
Paradise Lost

Babb, Lawrence. *The Moral Cosmos of* Paradise Lost. East
Lansing: Michigan State University Press, 1970.

Berry, Boyd M. *Process of Speech: Puritan Religious Writing
and* Paradise Lost. Baltimore: Johns Hopkins University Press,
1976.

Blessington, Frances C. Paradise Lost *and the Classical Epic.*
London: Routledge & Kegan Paul, 1979.

Bloom, Harold, ed. *John Milton.* New York: Chelsea House,
1986.

————, ed. *John Milton's* Paradise Lost. New York: Chelsea
House, 1987.

Bush, Douglas. Paradise Lost *in Our Time: Some Comments.*
Ithaca, NY: Cornell University Press, 1945.

Daniel, Clay. *Death in Milton's Poetry.* Lewisburg, PA: Bucknell
University Press, 1994.

Danielson, Dennis. *Milton's Good God: A Study in Literary
Theodicy.* Cambridge: Cambridge University Press, 1982.

————, ed. *The Cambridge Companion to Milton.* Cambridge:
Cambridge University Press, 1989.

Darbishire, Helen. *Milton's* Paradise Lost. Oxford: Clarendon
Press, 1951.

Demaray, John G. *Milton's Theatrical Epic: The Invention and
Design of* Paradise Lost. Cambridge, MA: Harvard University
Press, 1980.

Evans, John Martin. Paradise Lost *and the Genesis Tradition.*
Oxford: Clarendon Press, 1968.

Fish, Stanley. *Surprised by Sin: The Reader in* Paradise Lost.
New York: St. Martin's Press, 1967.

Frye, Northrop. *The Return to Eden: Five Essays on Milton's Epics.* Toronto: University of Toronto Press, 1965.

Fuller, Elizabeth Ely. *Milton's Kinesthetic Vision in* Paradise Lost. Lewisburg, PA: Bucknell University Press, 1983.

Gardner, Helen L. *A Reading of* Paradise Lost. Oxford: Clarendon Press, 1965.

Gregory, E. R. *Milton and the Muses.* Tuscaloosa: University of Alabama Press, 1989.

Grossman, Marshall. *Authors to Themselves: Milton and the Revelation of History.* Cambridge: Cambridge University Press, 1987.

Guillory, John. *Poetic Authority: Spenser, Milton, and Literary History.* New York: Columbia University Press, 1983.

Kendrick, Christopher. *Milton: A Study in Ideology and Form.* New York: Methuen, 1986.

Kermode, Frank. *The Living Milton.* London: Routledge & Kegan Paul, 1960.

Knott, John Ray. *Milton's Pastoral Vision.* Chicago: University of Chicago Press, 1971.

Le Comte, Edward. *Milton and Sex.* New York: Columbia University Press, 1978.

Leonard, John. *Naming in* Paradise Lost: *Milton and the Language of Adam and Eve.* Oxford: Oxford University Press, 1990.

Lieb, Michael. *Milton and the Culture of Violence.* Ithaca, NY: Cornell University Press, 1994.

———. *Poetics of the Holy: A Reading of* Paradise Lost. Chapel Hill: University of North Carolina Press, 1981.

McCallum, Hugh. *Milton and the Sons of God: The Divine Image in Milton's Epic Poetry.* Toronto: University of Toronto Press, 1986.

Marjara, Harinder Singh. *Contemplation of Created Things: Science in* Paradise Lost. Toronto: University of Toronto Press, 1992.

Martindale, Charles. *John Milton and the Transformation of Ancient Epic.* Totowa, NJ: Barnes & Noble, 1986.

Martz, Louis L. *Milton, Poet of Exile.* 2nd ed. New Haven: Yale University Press, 1986.

Milner, Andrew. *Milton and the English Revolution.* London: Macmillan, 1981.

Moore, Leslie E. *Beautiful Sublime: The Making of* Paradise Lost *1701–1734.* Stanford: Stanford University Press, 1990.

Newlyn, Lucy. Paradise Lost *and the Romantic Reader.* Oxford: Clarendon Press, 1993.

Patrides, C. A. *Milton and the Christian Tradition.* Oxford: Clarendon Press, 1966.

Porter, William M. *Reading the Classics and* Paradise Lost. Lincoln: University of Nebraska Press, 1993.

Revard, Stella P. *The War in Heaven:* Paradise Lost *and the Tradition of Satan's Rebellion.* Ithaca, NY: Cornell University Press, 1980.

Riggs, William G. *The Christian Poet in* Paradise Lost. Berkeley: University of California Press, 1972.

Rosenblatt, Jason P. *Torah and Law in* Paradise Lost. Princeton: Princeton University Press, 1994.

Schulman, Lydia Dittler. Paradise Lost *and the Rise of the American Republic.* Boston: Northeastern University Press, 1992.

Schwartz, Regina M. *Remembering and Repeating: Biblical Creation in* Paradise Lost. Cambridge: Cambridge University Press, 1988.

Shawcross, John T. *With Mortal Voice: The Creation of* Paradise Lost. Lexington: University Press of Kentucky, 1982.

Steadman, John M. *Milton's Biblical and Classical Imagery.* Pittsburgh: Duquesne University Press, 1984.

Stein, Arnold. *The Art of Presence: The Poet and* Paradise Lost. Berkeley: University of California Press, 1977.

Stevens, Paul. *Imagination and the Presence of Shakespeare in* Paradise Lost. Madison: University of Wisconsin Press, 1985.

Summers, Joseph H. *The Muse's Method: An Introduction to* Paradise Lost. Cambridge, MA: Harvard University Press, 1962.

Swaim, Kathleen M. *Before and After the Fall: Contrasting Modes in* Paradise Lost. Amherst: University of Massachusetts Press, 1986.

Waldock, A. J. A. Paradise Lost *and Its Critics.* Cambridge: Cambridge University Press, 1947.

Walker, Julia M., ed. *Milton and the Idea of Woman.* Urbana: University of Illinois Press, 1988.

Index of
Themes and Ideas